Remember Who You Are
Baptism, a Model for Christian Life

Remember Who You Are

Baptism, a Model for Christian Life

William H. Willimon

UPPER
ROOM BOOKS®
NASHVILLE

Cover Design: David Uttley/D2 Design
Cover Photograph: Image Bank/Steve McAlister
Illustrations: Bruce Sayre
Eleventh Printing: 2004

Library of Congress Catalog Card Number: 79-93359
ISBN: 0-8358-0399-6

Printed in the United States of America

For
Harriet and William
who everyday remind me who I am

Contents

Introduction

Yonder is the sea, great and wide,
which teems with things innumerable. —*Psalm 104:25*

I write this while sitting upon the porch of an old beach house overlooking the Carolina coast. It is early morning, the water is calm, the sun has climbed out of the sea, a new day is beginning, rising for the billionth time out of those eternal waters.

Out of that restless, churning, ceaselessly rolling sea, life itself was begun millions of years ago. The sea still supports life. Humankind is as dependent upon the sea's gifts as we have ever been, ecologists remind us. And every time life is conceived in the waters of the womb, a new human being recapitulates the whole creation process again—the gift of life emerging from the waters of life.

This is a book about the Christian life, therefore it is a book about Christian baptism, therefore it is a book about water—about the "water and the word" of baptism, to be exact. It is written from the conviction that in a Christian's baptism we see the mode and the model for a Christian's life. When someone asked Martin Luther, "How do I know I am a Christian?" the salty old pastor replied, "You know you are baptized—that's all you need to know." A Christian is someone who by "water and the word" has begun to live the death and resurrection of Jesus in his or her own life. It is that simple and obvious, and yet it is also that strange and complex.

This is a book for those who want to explore the meaning of the gift of their baptism and its significance for daily life. These

9

thoughts about baptism are part historical, part biblical, part theological, part personal, and all devotional. I have organized them in such a way as to be of use to church school classes, study groups, prayer groups, and others who wish to view baptism as the starting point for reflection upon what it means to be a disciple to today's world. I hope this book will also be helpful to parents who are preparing to have a child baptized, pastors preparing to baptize someone or to instruct someone about baptism, and for newly baptized adults who want to know what happens to them when they pass through the waters.

My thanks to my parishioners, students, and friends who first heard and responded to these thoughts while they were in the process of development. Thanks to the good folk of First United Methodist Church, Conway, South Carolina, whom I served on Sundays while I wrote this book, managing even to baptize a few of their young. Thanks to Bruce Sayre for the illustrations and to John Westerhoff for the educational guides.

Thanks also to the late Reverend Grady Forrester who, on one hot, summer Sunday afternoon in my dim past, took me in his arms, held me over a silver bowl, poured water over my bald head, called me by name, and told me I was a Christian. About thirty summers later, in spite of what I have done and where I have been, that graceful water still fills my shoes, those words still thunder in my brain, and I still answer to that name—and it all came to me as a gift.

WILL WILLIMON
Advent, 1979

An Educational Introduction

Remember Who You Are is one of those rare books which deserves to be read and studied by every adult in the church. Few issues are more crucial for the future of the church and its faith than baptism. Few issues are more controversial. Differences of opinion and practice have existed throughout the history of the church. Today misunderstandings abound; confusion reigns. Of all the issues which adults might address, baptism may be the most important. William Willimon has penned a readable, theologically sound, stimulating introduction for persons who want to understand baptism—the church's rite of initiation—and to make baptism in their church more meaningful. I count it a privilege to recommend it to you and a pleasure to be given the opportunity to write an educational guide for its use.

Christians have always agreed that Christians are made, not born, and that baptism is intended for committed adults or for committed adults and their children. I personally am among those who advocate baptism for persons no younger than their young adult years—that is, about twenty-two—after systematic instruction and formation in three stages for a year or more by the Christian community.

During the first stage, persons attend inquiry classes which are designed to help them determine if they wish to make the serious and awesome decision to become a Christian. It is a time during which those who have been initially attracted to the Christian community are guided to examine and test their motives, in order that they may freely commit themselves to pursue a disciplined, lengthy exploration of the implications of Christian living. During the second stage, along with sponsors appointed by the church, persons are to attend regularly the worship of the community, receive encouragement and guidance in the life of prayer, acquire a personal knowledge of the history of salvation as revealed in the holy scriptures and, through acts of Christian service and action, practice life in accordance with the gospel. Following this period of preparation, when the community believes that they are ready, persons are baptized and receive their first communion. Thus, they enter the third stage of their instruction, a period during which the newly baptized, through formal and informal means, are assisted to experience the fullness of corporate life in the community of faith and to gain a deeper understanding of the sacraments and their implications for faithful life in the world.

Now while I personally believe that adult baptism and lengthy adult preparation are normative for the church, many Christians (Professor Willimon and myself among them) believe that the baptism of babies is a legitimate practice *if* at least one of the parents is a faithful, communing, baptized Christian and if this person(s) is willing to engage in a significant and lengthy period of preparation, with sponsors or godparents approved by the church, in prayer, reflection of their own baptismal covenant, and participation in acts of Christian service and action.

All of this sounds strange, I suspect, to most people who have begun to read this book. We have not always taken baptism that seriously. Part of the problem is that we have not fully understood the nature of this important rite. That is the reason for this book. If baptism is to regain its historic significance, we need to study seriously its meaning.

This book was written to stimulate and enhance learning and spiritual growth. There are a host of ways it might be used. Minimally, all adults, especially those who are considering baptism for themselves or their children, might read and reflect upon it alone and with their pastor. Others might choose to read it thoughtfully, making notes in the margins in the form of agreements, disagreements, questions, and the like to be shared with one or more other adults on a single occasion or over a period of time. Another possibility has been built into the content of the book itself. At the beginning of each chapter are suggestions for activities to be completed before reading the chapter. At the close of the chapter are other suggestions for reflection. At the end of the book, there is an educational guide for groups in the church who might choose to use the book as a basis for their corporate learning.

While baptism is an unrepeatable rite, it is both proper and necessary for each of us continually to renew our baptismal covenant. Baptism is best understood as a communal event, especially appropriate at Easter reminding us of death and rebirth, on the Day of Pentecost reminding us of the gift of the Holy Spirit, on All Saint's Day or the Sunday after All Saint's Day reminding us of our fellowship in the communion of the saints and membership in the church, and on the feast of the Baptism of our Lord (the first Sunday after Epiphany) reminding us of our call to ministry. On these occasions whether or not there are any persons to be baptized we each are called upon to renew our baptism.

This book can serve as a spiritual resource for the personal renewal of our faith and life as believers in Jesus Christ and members of his church. My hope is that every church will find a way to make this book a resource for its reflection on the nature and meaning of baptism as the model for the Christian life. Professor Willimon has combined scholarship with a lively, thought-provoking, and challenging style. It is without reservation and indeed with enthusiasm that I commend its use throughout the church.

John H. Westerhoff III
Professor of Religion and Education
Duke University Divinity School
Advent, 1979

1. The Rock from Whence You Were Hewn

Before you read this chapter, take a few moments to write a description of a baptismal service as it is typically celebrated in your church.

You are no longer strangers and sojourners, but you are fellow citizens with the saints and members of the household of God.—Eph. 2:19

I

We are in ancient Rome.[1] It is almost dawn. The streets of the great city are beginning to stir with the first life of a Sunday morning. A vendor trudges through the pre-dawn darkness, making his way down the street to the Forum where he will peddle his wares. On his way, he stumbles on a paving stone and falls before the steps of a large Roman home. He curses Jove as he picks himself up. Brushing off his tunic, in the silence of the deserted street, he hears the faint sound of people singing. He stops and listens, putting his ear to the massive front door of the house. He cannot see anything over the large wall which separates the house from the street, but he can hear singing—singing, at this hour of the day—even though he cannot make out the words. Probably some late night revelry, some drunken dinner party which has lasted all evening, he thinks to himself.

"The gods make some to eat and drink and feast all night so they can sleep all day. The rest of us poor souls are made only for work," he mutters as he rights his cart and pushes it down the street in darkness.

The vendor could not know that behind the door a feast was beginning rather than ending. Behind the locked door, safe from the intrusion of hostile government authorities, a group of people were gathering to celebrate the secret rites of an illegal religion. They were Christians, come to celebrate what they called *Pascha,* Easter, the most joyful day of their joyful faith. Today they would

15

receive new converts into their gathering, receiving them through a strange rite of initiation which they called "baptism."

Let us open that door, closed for centuries, and observe these earliest Christians and their baptism, their rite of initiation.

II

The door opens and we enter. We stand in the *atrium* or colonnaded court of a typical Roman home. In the courtyard, a group of people sit at the feet of an older man who gives them instruction. All is darkness, save the light of one small lamp by which the man reads from a scroll.

The people being instructed are called *catechumens* ("hearers"). These catechumens are now in the last stage of what has been a three-year period of preparation for participation in the church. They are being instructed by one who is called an *episcopos* ("bishop" or "overseer"). It is the duty of the episcopos to guide the catechumens through this arduous process of instruction and examination. It is now his duty to examine each catechumen to decide if he or she is at last ready to be initiated into the church.

Long before this night, the candidates have been carefully examined by the congregation's elders to see if they are worthy to begin the process of instruction and initiation. Even though the church is now persecuted by the government, fighting for its very life, the church is careful to define itself against its pagan environment. All those who seek admission are rigorously examined. Idolaters, actors, circus performers, pimps, gladiators, harlots, astrologers, and magicians are rejected outright because of the immoral and pagan connotations of these amusements. Soldiers and high government officials are also rejected—unless they will take certain vows of allegiance—because of their subservience to the pagan state. Artists and teachers, notorious dabblers in pagan myths and fables, are only hesitatingly accepted. In other words, the church sets a high cost, demands a decisive break with the pagan world, an either-or response to its claims. Either one must be determined to be a whole Christian, or one must be no Christian at all. Like the rich young ruler before Christ (Luke 18:23), many go away sad because they are unwilling to pay the price.

For those who are admitted as catechumens, a three-year period of instruction and worship follows. The three-year period is

16

primarily a time of moral trial in which the catechumen's life is disciplined to comply with the ethical expectations of the church. In other words, entrance into the church involves "conversion," a turning around of one's life-style, personal habits, and point of view until all is disciplined to the rule of faith. Catechumens are allowed to attend the first part of Sunday worship, the Service of the Word, in which the scripture is read and a sermon preached. But they are dismissed before the Lord's Supper, usually with a prayer and a blessing.

After three years, catechumens who prove themselves by their lives are examined. Do they honor the widows, visit the sick, and fulfill good work? Those who pass this examination are admitted as *competentes* ("candidates"). A few weeks before Easter, the instruction of these candidates changes from moral instruction to teaching about the gospel. The Apostle's Creed is explained to them as a brief summary of essential truth for the Christian. Candidates fast and participate in night-watches or vigils. The bishop frequently pronounces exorcisms over them during these last days so that Satan's power over their lives is gradually weakened.

Finally, as Holy Week approached, the catechumens have washed themselves daily in preparation for baptism. Friday night (known as "Good Friday" to us) and Saturday before Easter have been spent in a strict fast. On Easter Eve, the candidates kept a vigil, listening to the scriptures and final instruction. As the first rays of light strike the horizon on this Easter Sunday morning, one by one, the candidates are led across the dark courtyard to a separate baptismal room of the house-church. The rite of Christian initiation has at last begun.

III

The baptismal room is a room of the house which has been set aside for this special purpose. Children are baptized first, with their parents or other relatives responding for them and leading them through the rite if they are too young to respond for themselves. Next, men are baptized, then women. Drucilla, a young servant woman, waits her time for baptism. At last she hears her name called, and she approaches the door. A deacon opens the door and bids her enter.

Flickering lamps illuminate the dark interior, revealing to her a series of simple drawings on the walls. Drucilla recognizes the pictures as biblical scenes which relate to baptism: Jesus walking upon the water, calling to the disciples who watched him from a boat; Moses striking the rock in the wilderness to bring forth water; Noah and his family in the ark; and others. Suddenly these stories begin to take on new meaning for her. *She* is now venturing out upon the uncertain waters of faith. *She* feels new life surging forth within her. *She* is being preserved in the church, safe from the destruction and death in a dying world.

A deaconess helps Drucilla remove all her clothing and jewelry. "Let nothing alien go into the water. Nothing from your old life must be preserved," the bishop had said. The deaconess leads her to the end of the room where she stands, naked as the day of her birth, before a boxlike pool which resembles a tomb. Prompted by an elder of the congregation, Drucilla makes a final dramatic renunciation: "I renounce you, Satan, and all your servants, and all your works."

She is then anointed with the "oil of exorcism," as the elder cries, "Let every evil spirit depart from you." The oil, which Romans use for cleansing purposes, signifies Drucilla's final purification from all the affections, allegiances, and standards of her former life.

Now, at last, Drucilla steps into the cold, deep waters of the font, led by a deaconess. The deaconess pushes her under the water as an elder asks her, "Do you believe in God?"

"I believe in God, the Father Almighty," affirms Drucilla.

"Do you believe in Jesus Christ?"

"I believe in Jesus Christ, his only Son our Lord." The deaconess submerges her again.

"Do you believe in the Holy Spirit?"

"I believe." A third and final time, Drucilla goes under the water.

She is now anointed with the "oil of thanksgiving." Then she dries herself, puts on her clothes, and follows a deacon down a narrow hallway which leads into the large banquet hall of the house. Here, with lamps burning brightly, all the faithful are gathered. She realizes that she is in the eucharistic hall of the church, the place where the sacred meal is celebrated. Everyone stands, smiling at Drucilla. She is immediately led to the bishop

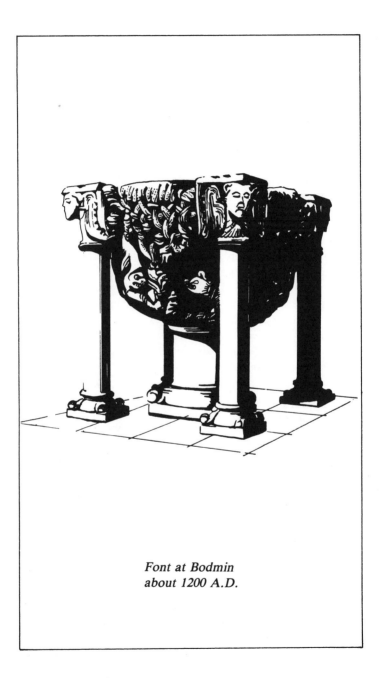

*Font at Bodmin
about 1200 A.D.*

who sits at the end of the room. Drucilla kneels before him as he lays his hands upon her head and prays this prayer,

> Lord God, who hast made Drucilla worthy to obtain remission of sins through the washing of regeneration of the Holy Spirit, send into her your grace, that she may serve you according to your will; for yours is glory, to the Father and the Son with the Holy Spirit in the holy church, both now and world without end. Amen.

Hearing the bishop's prayer, feeling the weight of his gentle hands upon her head, Drucilla truly feels that she had been cleansed, reborn, filled with a new life-giving Spirit this day.

Now the bishop takes a small bottle of oil and anoints her a third time with the "oil of thanksgiving," saying, "I anoint you with holy oil in the Lord, the Father Almighty, and Christ Jesus and the Holy Ghost." He now makes the sign of the cross upon her forehead, "the seal of the Spirit," marking her, branding her as a disciple of Christ. He then kisses Drucilla and presents her to the surrounding assembly.

"Greet your new sister in Christ," the bishop proclaims. Everyone surges forward to embrace Drucilla and welcome her into the congregation.

For the first time, Drucilla and the other new Christians are able to join the congregation in prayer—a privilege which had been withheld until they were initiated. After the prayers of intercession, everyone gathers around a large table. The deacons collect jugs of wine and loaves of bread from everyone for the meal. Drucilla feels privileged to be able to offer her loaf of home-baked bread for the first time. It is placed on the table with the rest of the offering. The bishop extends his hands over the table and begins a long prayer of thanksgiving. Drucilla's excitement grows at the thought of at last being able to join in the Lord's Supper with the rest of her fellow Christians.

As she prays, Drucilla looks up at the high windows of the room. They are aglow with the first light of morning. The new day has begun, Easter Sunday has come, the Resurrection day is here. For Drucilla it is as if she has died and has been raised on this day. A new light has dawned in her own life.

After everyone has eaten bread and drunk wine, the bishop

leads in singing a hymn, a hymn which says what Drucilla has experienced on this wonderful day:

> The Father, who has qualified us to share in the inheritance of the saints in light. He has delivered us from the dominion of darkness and transferred us to the kingdom of his beloved Son, in whom we have redemption, the forgiveness of sins.
>
> (Col. 1:12-14)

Then, after a blessing by the bishop, everyone embraces and leaves for home, hurrying down the streets in the early morning light, dispersing quickly lest the authorities be alerted about this suspicious gathering. Drucilla hurries home, too, conscious that she might pay a high price for her new faith. But she is willing to suffer all cost, because this day she has received something which is without price.

IV

We have just had a glimpse of baptism as it might have taken place in a house-church in Rome in the second century. I have reconstructed this episode for you, not to suggest that we ought to do baptism in this fashion today, nor, on the other hand, to open with a little history lesson. I show you this baptismal rite in order to let you see something of the earliest roots of baptism. This is the "rock from whence you were hewn," the way the earliest Christians made new Christians.

These are our roots, our spiritual forebears. While we cannot, probably should not, try to imitate their worship practices, I cannot help comparing this early account of baptism with the way baptism is done today. A young mother phones the church office and asks to have her new baby "done" next Sunday. One of the baby's aunts will be in town that weekend and it would be nice to have her there. The pastor hesitates for a few moments before responding, since he only sees the baby's mother in church occasionally and has yet to meet the father whom the mother describes as "not the church going type." But, since everybody will be in town this weekend and since the pastor feels that he could not begin to explain to the couple why he feels uncomfortable baptizing their baby, the pastor agrees to ''do'' the baby during next Sunday's service.

''We're already having a rather full service next Sunday because we're in the middle of our fall stewardship emphasis and the choir has planned two anthems. Maybe we ought simply to do it after the service rather than unduly prolong things,'' says the pastor. ''Oh well, we can wedge the sprinkling in during the first part of the service—before the baby gets restless. You bring her on down Sunday.'' The preceding is a glimpse of baptism as it might have taken place in a suburban church in the United States in the late twentieth century.

When I make a comparison between these two baptismal accounts, the following characteristics of baptism in the early church strike me at first glance.

1. The church assumed that one could not be a Christian without conversion, instruction, and a general reorientation of one's life. The goal of that complex and arduous three-year catechumenate was *conversion*—nothing less than complete, thorough-going conversion into a totally new creation. As Tertullian said, ''Christians are made, not born.'' No one becomes a Christian by birthright. God has no grandchildren. Each of us must be reborn, re-created, remade, changed.

2. Baptism, in this account of the early church, is not a momentary rite wedged into a Sunday service. Baptism is both the culmination—the recapitulation of a long *process* of conversion and nurture—and the beginning of a long *process* of conversion and nurture.

3. Baptism is *Christian initiation*. The goal of this process and its culminating rite is not some individualized, purely personal experience. The goal of baptism is initiation into a community of faith, a church. It is entrance into a way of life together, not a private rite to do something to or for individuals in private. It asserts from its beginning that to be a follower of Christ means to be grafted into the Body of Christ. There is no Christian without church, no faith outside the community of faith.

4. Christian initiation and its attendant rite of baptism is the *proper and primary business of the church*. The church has

been told to make disciples by "baptizing and teaching" (Matt. 28:19-20). Our major work is the evangelistic business of claiming people for the Kingdom and fitting them for life in that Kingdom. Baptism is that rich, multi-faceted, complex way of engaging the body, head, and heart in that strange and glorious work of claiming, instructing, washing, anointing, blessing, and receiving people for the Kingdom.

Perhaps you can add others. Obviously, when these assertions are compared with most of our current baptismal practices, it is readily apparent that most of our churches have much work to do in regard to the way they equip and nurture Christians. The work the church needs to do is important, because in baptism we have the basis of the church and the origin and goal of the Christian life. But the first step to reform is to understand what baptism is, what it means, and what it does. Only then will we know how we, some nineteen centuries after the world of those first Christians, are to convert and equip Christians in our world.

For now, let our encounter with our baptismal past guide us as we explore the significance of baptism for our present and future life in Christ.

Compare and contrast baptism as you described it in your church with that of the early church. How are they similar and different? Make a list of your questions about the nature and meaning of baptism. Hazard a preliminary answer to your questions.

---

2. Royalty

Every child asks "Who am I"? Write for some imagined child, your answer to this question.

You are a chosen race, a royal priesthood, a holy nation, God's own people. —1 Pet. 2:9

I

Who first told me? Who first told you? Who first said that you were a wretched offender, miserable sinner, no good? Was it your parents, when they first shook you and scolded you and told you to behave? Or your teachers, when they told you to go to the bottom of the class? Or your boss, when he asked you to do it over and try to get it right this time? Or your children, who looked at you and judged you to be parentally inadequate? Or did they all tell you? They all told you who you are. You are the over-drinking, over-spending, over-sexed, under-achieving, under-giving, under-loving, worm-like one who is not quite what the Creator has in mind when he thinks of "the image of God."

"All, like sheep, have gone astray," cries the prophet. "All have sinned and fallen short of the glory of God," laments Paul. "Every corner of my heart is a cage of unclean birds," says the venerable St. Bernard. Even one so noble as Augustine, for all his belief in the grace of God, died in tears and terror, eyes fixed upon the penitential psalms. We have all learned well this litany of self-condemnation, taught to us by a world which at every turn reminded us of our miserable, wretched state.

The traditional baptismal service in the old *Book of Common Prayer* welcomes the candidate to the font with these cheerful words, "For as much as all men have sinned and fallen short of the glory of God. Our Savior Christ said, 'Unless one is born of water and the Spirit, he cannot enter the kingdom of God.'"

In other words, you are no good. This is who you are. You have some primal defect in you which we must now labor to correct at the font. But I know another song which is older than this mournful litany of condemnation and degradation. It was sung at the church's first baptisms, and it is a far cry from our familiar refrain of human unworthiness:

> But you are a chosen race, a royal priesthood, a holy nation, God's own people, that you may declare the wonderful deeds of him who called you out of darkness into his marvelous light. Once you were no people but now you are God's people; once you had not received mercy but now you have received mercy (1 Pet. 2:9-10).

I heard a similar song as Jesse Jackson began worship in his inner-city Chicago congregation. Jackson had the entire church shout with him in unison,

> I was nobody.
> But now, thank God, I'm *somebody!*

There, in the midst of economic and racial oppression, when the whole world told these people that they were nothing but nobodies, the church dared to be different and belligerently shout forth that as God's cherished children they were *somebodies*.

Who tells you who you are?

II

While baptism primarily involved water as the essential sign-act of the sacrament, baptism traditionally has used additional actions to underscore its meaning. From our description of a first-century baptism in chapter one, you probably noted the use, throughout the rite, of oil. In these early rites, oil was used for the same two purposes for which it was used throughout the ancient world: cleansing and anointing.

The ancients used oil like we use soap or perfume, rubbing it over their bodies before and after bathing. In the early baptismal rites, the "oil of exorcism" fulfilled this function, cleansing an individual as preparation for initiation into the church.

Oil was also used as a sign of consecration or designation. In the Old Testament, priests, prophets, and kings were consecrated and set apart by anointing. The office of priest, prophet, or king was viewed as a ministry, a service to God and God's people. The anointings made someone God's representative, giving that person special endowments and gifts to fulfill that service. (See 1 Sam. 16:13; Isa. 61:1.) As the specially designated and endowed one, the anointed one was also the recipient of God's protection and care. God's "seal" was upon him or her. "Thou anointest my head with oil, my cup overflows," sings the psalmist (23:5).

All of this is of interest to Christians, because in the New Testament Jesus is called *the* "anointed one," the "Messiah." *Messiah* is the Hebrew word for "the anointed" (*Christos* in Greek). He is the one whom God "anointed ... with the Holy Spirit and with power" (Acts 10:38). In Luke's Gospel (4:18), Jesus applies Isa. 61:1-2 to himself, telling the folk at Nazareth that "the Lord ... has anointed me to preach good news to the poor." Jesus is the *Christos-Messiah,* the Christ. As the anointed one, he is priest, prophet, and king, "anointed" at his baptism when the Spirit descends upon him and declares to all, "Thou art my beloved Son; with thee I am well pleased" (Luke 3:22).

Even if Jesus is the Christ, the Messiah, the anointed, what does that have to do with us? Paul makes the astounding assertion that "God . . . establishes us with you in Christ, and has commissioned (literally, 'anointed') us; he has put his seal upon us ('seal' being the technical term for baptism in the early church) and given us his Spirit in our hearts as a guarantee" (2 Cor. 1:21-22). In other words, everyone who is baptized in the name of Christ is anointed and sealed like Christ to share in Christ's threefold activity of priest, prophet, and king.

This is what that baptismal hymn in 1 Peter 2:9-10 is all about. When it declared to the baptized, "You are a chosen race, a royal priesthood, a holy nation," it was only echoing what had been said to Israel centuries before. Israel had been chosen "above all peoples" (Deut. 10:15) and had been delivered from slavery so that she could be "a kingdom of priests and a holy nation" (Exod. 19:6). Israel was chosen, signed, sealed, and anointed to be a holy nation of priests, prophets, and kings.

Now, through baptism, even Gentiles can be admitted to the status of Israel. Even Gentiles can now be set apart for God's priestly, prophetic, kingly work. As Christ, *the* royal one, delivers them, these royal ones are commissioned to deliver others, to

26

"declare the wonderful deeds of him who called you out of darkness into his marvelous light" (1 Pet. 2:9).

All that baptismal ceremonial which was described in chapter one—the bath, the changing of clothes, the anointing and laying on of hands, followed by eating and drinking—corresponds directly to Old Testament patterns for the initiation of *priests*. Baptism is as much consecration as it is initiation. In other words, baptism is each Christian's *ordination* into the priesthood of Christ, each Christian's commissioning to share in Christ's work in the world.

What is that work? At an early date, the church began giving a lighted candle to the newly baptized with the words, "You are the light of the world. Let your light shine." The work of the Christian is primarily evangelistic work. At your baptism you are anointed and set apart that you may "declare the wonderful deeds of him who called you out of darkness into his marvelous light."

It is strange that most of us Protestants have dropped the practice of anointing with oil at baptism. Orthodox, Roman Catholic, Anglican, and some Lutheran Christians still use the sweet smelling oil, called *chrism,* at their baptisms. It is strange that many of us do not anoint at baptism, since Protestants hold dear the doctrine of the "priesthood of all believers." No activity could make that baptismal ordination into the ministry of Christ more clear than the pouring of oil on someone's head accompanied by the words, "You are now God's priest, prophet, king! This is who you are!"

III

Who tells you who you are: Your parents, your children, your nation, your job, your friends, your school, your bank account? If you allow others to tell you who you are, they will be only too happy to tell you. But that is a dangerous way.

Through baptism, a Christian first and finally learns who he or she is. It is the rite of identity. Baptism asserts rather than argues, it proclaims rather than explains, it commands rather than requests, it acts rather than signifies, and it involves rather than describes. When you ask in desperation, "Who, in God's name, am I?" baptism will have you feel the water dripping from your head and the oil oozing down your neck and say, "You are, in

God's name, *royalty,* God's own, claimed and ordained for God's serious and joyful business. So, therefore, you had better get with it."

Part of our present trouble with baptism, and with living as Christians, is that we have misplaced the action of baptism. Like almost everyone else in our modern world, we Christians have put too much stress on *human* doubts, strivings, misdeeds, questions, aspirations, and too little stress upon *God.* In our Sunday worship, we incessantly chatter about human sin, human problems, human questions, human feelings. We tirelessly reiterate and catalog all the evidences of human frailty and falsehood. We tell people to get out there and start living right or thinking right or feeling right. We present the Christian faith as an achievement, a goal, an attainment of sincere and struggling sinners who are earnestly trying to get right with God. This all sounds reasonable in our self-help, achievement-oriented society. But it does not sound like Good News. The Good News says that we do not need to "get right with God." The gospel says we *are* right with God. We do not need to work to get anywhere. We have arrived. We are not miserable wretches inching our way into God's good graces. We are royalty who already have assigned seats in the Kingdom—by God's grace.

This is all ours, not because we are "basically good people after all," not even because (as we have been told in many sermons) we are basically bad people who must admit we are bad, start living right, and thereby make ourselves good. We are who we are by *God's* grace. God's *grace.* We are not "basically good people." We know that better than anybody else. And we are at our worst when we anxiously strive to be "basically good people." This ends in all kinds of games, deceits, and boasting, which are the result of all religion which bases itself on "works righteousness"—religion which tries to "get right with God" rather than relying only upon God's loving righteousness. We are who we are because *God* has loved us, chosen us, adopted us, anointed us for his own.

We have clouded the Good News with a bunch of "oughts": You *ought* to love others. You *ought* to live a better life. You *ought* to grow up and act your age. You *ought* to give yourself to God. Baptism says little about what you ought to be or do. It mainly asserts who you *are:* You *are* a new people. You *are* a holy nation. You *are* royalty so you might as well get used to it. The imperative, "you ought," comes only after the indicative, "You are."

It makes all the difference in the world whether we conceive of being Christian as something which we *ought* to do or as something which we *are*. When a father tells his son, "make something out of yourself," he is implying that the boy is not worth much as he is. It would be better for the father to sit down with the boy and tell him that his parents love him, believe in him, and have great plans for his future. Then the boy's behavior would arise from a desire to be who he is rather than from a fear of what he might become. Baptism does not say, "You can be God's own *if* you do this or believe that." Baptism says, "You *are* God's own with no doubts at all."

In the New Testament, whenever the meaning of baptism is interpreted to people who are about to be baptized, it is always spoken of in the future tense, in terms of promises about a new identity. So, to the crowd who asked, "What must we do to be saved?" Peter says, "Repent, and be baptized, and you shall receive the Holy Spirit because this promise is to you and your children" (Acts 2:37-39, my paraphrase).

When baptism is interpreted to those who have been baptized, it is spoken of in the past tense, as a biographical fact of life. A change has happened. God has done something to you. You are somebody special, a new creation (1 Pet. 2:9-10).

All of us must take our cue from baptism and do less talking about what people ought to do or be and do more proclamation of who people *are*. Typical of the problem is our recent dealing with the rite of confirmation. Confirmation is historically a part of the baptismal rite. We usually explain confirmation by saying that it provides a time for an adolescent to "publically confirm his or her faith," "accept Jesus Christ as Savior," or worse (in light of what baptism means), "join the church." This talk about confirmation is curious since it all speaks of actions, decisions, and intentions of the person being confirmed. Historically, confirmation was viewed from the other side. The *church* confirmed the person, or *God* confirmed the faith of the person. We once told a person in confirmation, in effect, "In case you didn't get the message at your baptism, we'll say it again, 'You are one of us. You are royalty. You are set apart. This is who you are.' ''

How typical of modern life for us to put the shoe on the other foot and view faith, identity, and salvation as something we do, as an achievement rather than a gift. Baptism says otherwise.

The church is not saying that someone is not a child of God until he or she is baptized. We are saying that it is difficult for a person to know that he or she is a child of God until he or she is baptized. The coronation of Queen Elizabeth did not "make" Elizabeth a Queen. A coronation can only make someone a queen if that person is already royalty. The nation said publicly at the coronation, "This woman is royalty, put a crown on her head." At baptism the church says publically, "This person is royalty, baptize her."

It is tragic for a couple to say they are anxious to have their baby baptized "lest something happen to her." This shows a misunderstanding of who the baby is and what baptism is. We do not baptize people to protect them from hell. We baptize them because of the Good News that they should know they belong to God. What greater or more pressing (or more joyful) work could the church be doing today than its baptismal work?

In my book *The Gospel for the Person Who Has Everything,* I tell about a young friend of mine, age four, who was asked on the occasion of his fifth birthday what kind of party he wanted to have.

"I want everyone to be a king or a queen," Clayton said.

So, he and his mother went to work fashioning a score of silver crowns (cardboard and aluminum foil), purple robes (crepe paper), and royal scepters (a stick painted gold). On the day of the party, as the guests arrived, they were each given their royal crown, robe, and scepter and were thus dressed as a king or queen. It was a regal sight—all kings and queens. Everyone had a wonderful time. They all ate ice cream and cake. Then they had a procession up to the end of the block and back again. All in all, it was a royal, wonderful day.

That evening, as Clayton's mom was tucking him into bed, she asked him what he wished when he blew the candles out on his birthday cake.

"I wished," he said, "that *everyone* in the whole world could be a king or queen—not just on my birthday, but *every* day."

Well, Clayton, baptism shows that something very much like that happened one day at a place called Calvary. We, who were nobodies, became somebodies. Those who were no people became God's people. The wretched of the earth became royalty.

Compare and contrast your original answer to the question "Who am I?" with the position presented in this chapter. How are they similar and different? If a child in your home or church were to experience himself or herself as "royalty," what would you and your church need to do more of and what would you need to do differently?

---

3. The Chosen

Answer the following questions: Who acts in a baptism? What do(es) the actor(s) do? Can a person be baptized more than once? Why or why not?

You did not choose me, but I chose you and appointed you that you should go and bear fruit and that your fruit should abide; so that whatever you ask the Father in my name, he may give it to you. —John 15:16

I

A friend of mine had a little brother who was caught in some misdeed by his father. When the boy's father confronted him with this wrong and threatened to punish him, the lad drew himself up to his full four-feet height and said proudly, "You can't touch me, I'm baptized!" Now there is a young man who knows the facts of life—as well as the facts of faith and baptism.

By this point it is clear that we are speaking of baptism in ways which many contemporary Christians have not heard before. How do we usually talk about baptism?

In one of my courses, I ask the seminarians to preach a baptismal sermon. I do this because I think sermons are a good way for pastors to help people grow in their understanding of baptism. But the typical baptismal sermon runs something like this: "Baptism is a rite which Jesus commanded us to do, but it means nothing *if* we do not understand what we are doing"; or, "While baptism is important, it is ineffective *unless* we bring our baptized child to Sunday school"; or, "Baptism means nothing *unless* we really feel it in our hearts"; or, "Baptism *means nothing* for the child; it is mainly a little service of dedication for the parents."

After a series of these sermons, I stand up in desperation and cry out, "Will anybody now tell me why Jesus would have been so thoughtless as to command us to do something so utterly ineffective and meaningless as baptism?" Most of us have spent our lives being told everything baptism does not do. In this book, I wish to say, as loudly and clearly as possible, what baptism does.

II

Our faulty thinking about baptism comes from forgetting what the church has always said: *Baptism is essentially something which God does.* For a long time, we Protestants have been in the grip of what James White has called an "Enlightenment view" of baptism. The eighteenth-century European Enlightenment deprecated the role of mystery in life. It sought to make all religion rational, reasonable, and understandable. Human understanding was stressed over divine activity. From this point of view, the question asked of sacraments like baptism is, "What does this mean to me, and what am I doing when this happens?" rather than, "What does this mean to God, and what is God doing when this happens?" We in the modern world are heirs of the Enlightenment. Enlightenment thought patterns were essential to the development of modern philosophy, psychology, and the sciences in general. But when these thought patterns were carried over into religion, the results were devastating.

We have been taught to think in Enlightenment terms for so long that we are unaware of how this manner of thinking shifts the entire focus of faith from God's actions to our actions. When the question has been asked, "What is baptism?" the Enlightenment response has been: Baptism is a ritual which is mainly of value in helping to remind us that God loves us. Baptism helps us understand certain truths. It helps the church remember to take responsibility for the baptized person. It is mostly of value in reminding parents to bring their child to church school and confirmation classes. In other words, baptism is essentially a little memory exercise for people, something which is chiefly of value in helping us to say, remember, or think something.

Pietists reacted against the Enlightenment's stress on pure reason with an equally misguided stress on pure feelings. Pietists stress that baptism is "an outward and visible sign" which means nothing unless we inwardly feel like a Christian. Our own feelings determine whether baptism "works" or not. If we do not feel it, it is not there. In other words, baptism is essentially a little stimulant to feeling. If asked, "What does baptism do?" both the heirs of the Enlightenment and the heirs of Pietism respond, "Well, it doesn't really *do* anything."

Both Pietism and the Enlightenment err in that they put all the action and meaning of baptism into purely human terms. They make baptism—as they made the rest of our worship—into a human-centered, human-conditioned, human-initiated activity. The person who says that she or he wants to be baptized again because, ''I didn't really understand what I was doing the first time I was baptized,'' is speaking from an understanding of baptism as something we think or feel. *Me,* my feelings, attitudes, beliefs, actions are the main fact of baptism or any other act of worship. God has nothing to do with it.

This view of baptism is not only heretical, but it also robs God's people of a primary means of God's gracious presence among them. It is heretical because the church has always asserted that *God* is the actor and we are the recipients of what God does through the sacraments. The saving work of God is not limited by or conditioned upon my feeling, understanding, or acting. The power of sacraments like baptism does not entirely depend upon me—my thoughts about God, my ability to love God, my feelings about myself or God, my skill at leading a holy life. In his infinite love, God has not left us alone. God continually, graciously, unconditionally gives himself to us and makes himself present to us in ways that can be touched, tasted, felt, seen, acted. As the psalmist puts it, ''Taste and see that the Lord is good'' (Psalm 34:8).

God knows we are earthlings, made of the stuff of earth—water, minerals, clay. Therefore God deals with us through earthly means. As John Calvin said, ''He condescends to lead us to himself by these earthly elements, and to set before us in the flesh a mirror of spiritual blessings. . . . he imparts spiritual things under visible ones'' (*Institutes of the Christian Religion,* Book IV, XIV, 3). This is the truth of all sacraments, including baptism: God using the stuff of everyday human life to give himself to us. Most of our baptismal rites suffer from a lack of water. Over the years, the waters of baptism were reduced from a bath to a mere trickle. No wonder baptism appears trivial and trite to many people. Let the graceful waters flow so that people will *see* and *feel* God's grace—not merely think about it.

If baptism is sign and seal of our salvation, if it is the door into the church, the path into the Kingdom, then baptism is first and foremost something which God does. My salvation is a work of

God. The church is a work of God, "his new creation by water and the word," as we sometimes sing. The Kingdom is a product of God which he calls forth and builds in his own good time. It is not the achievement of our social activism. God is always the primary actor in these matters. We are always the recipients of and the responders to God's loving, saving, redeeming, initiating, birthing action.

The Bible, Old and New Testaments, states that salvation is always God's work, not ours. Israel was "no people," a wandering tribe of desert nomads without claim to national grandeur or goodness. But God chose to make Israel a great name, a holy people, a blessing to all the nations. Why? The Bible does not answer that question except to suggest that it was some inscrutable mystery of divine love. Israel did nothing to earn that love. In fact, she did almost everything to betray and mock that love. And yet, through all her infidelity and waywardness, God still loved Israel, choosing her again and again to be a light to the Gentiles. Throughout the Old Testament story of Israel's ups and downs as the chosen people, the "hero" of the story, the main actor in the drama, is God. The Good News is that God chose Israel and continues to love Israel even though she chose to betray and reject that love.

The New Testament continues, expands, universalizes this Gospel drama of God's loving action in human history. The Gospel of John states explicitly what all the Gospels say implicitly: "You did not choose me, but I chose you" (John 15:16). Jesus came preaching Good News to the poor, the captives, the dispossessed, the blind, the sick, the heavy laden. All of these "little ones" were chosen precisely because they had no hope other than God. In Jesus, they not only heard but saw enacted the grace of God in their midst, God choosing the small rather than the great, the poor rather than the rich, the sick rather than the well. They were chosen, not because the small, the poor, the sick are better than others; they were chosen because God in Christ chose to be their God, placing himself on their side for all time.

I remember discussing the apostle Peter with a sixth-grade church school class one Sunday. We had studied how Peter never seemed to understand what Jesus was talking about. We discussed how Peter forsook Jesus and fled when the going got rough at the

Baptismal pool at Kelibia
3rd century

time of the crucifixion, and how Peter had to be rebuked by Paul for his narrow-mindedness. And yet, this was the man whom Jesus called "the rock," in recognition of Peter's faith. It was upon this faith that Jesus would build his church.

"What does that tell you about Jesus?" I asked.

"It tells me that Jesus was a lousy judge of character," said one of the sixth graders.

If we go through the Bible expecting to discover some noble personal attributes of nations or individual men and women which qualify them as deserving candidates for God's grace, we will be disappointed. That is not the point. The Bible speaks about the generous, gracious love of God who chooses *even* men and women like Peter upon whom to build his church.

Some people glorify biblical folk like Peter, extolling his courage, his insight, his faith, or some other alleged attribute, and telling us, "You ought to be like Peter." Be like Peter? Thick-headed? Impulsive? Cowardly? Prejudiced? God help us, we already *are* like Peter! And yet, God chooses *us*, even us, as the building blocks for his kingdom. Once again, the "hero" of the story is *God*.

III

There can be no more beautiful enactment, no more powerful statement of salvation as something which God does than baptism. In baptism, the recipient of baptism is just that—recipient. You cannot very well do your own baptism. It is done to you, for you.

Unfortunately, most of our past arguments about baptism show that when we discuss salvation or baptism we put the emphasis in the wrong place. Both the supporters of infant baptism and the advocates of adult baptism have too often focused upon the recipient of the sacrament rather than upon the chief actor in the sacrament. Infant baptism advocates have sometimes argued that "the child must be baptized in order to be saved," so that baptism becomes a magical rite which is the right of the child in order that the child will be protected from hell. Or, in more recent years, supporters of infant baptism have sometimes claimed that infant baptism is a valid practice, but valid only if it is followed by confirmation, at which time the baptized child is *really* received into the church. Opponents of infant baptism have complained that when a child is baptized, the child's freedom of choice is violated. They say that we should not baptize until the child is "old enough to know what it means" or until the child has "accepted Christ for himself or herself." In both cases, the focus is upon the rights, disposition, choices, feelings, and future of the recipient of baptism rather than upon God or God's church.

But if we believe that baptism, like our salvation in general, is essentially something *God* does, then this shifts the entire focus of our baptismal discussion and changes our questions. The questions cease being, "What must this person think or feel or believe or promise or do?" and become, "What does *God* think, feel, believe, do, and promise in baptism?" It is the *church* which was told to "Go, make disciples . . . baptizing . . . teaching." The *church* bears the task of making disciples, not individuals. Baptism is the church's proclamation and experience that we are who we are because *God* has first chosen us and loved us and called us into his Kingdom. The burden of baptism is more on the baptizers than the ones being baptized.

Sometimes I think that we in the church shift the burden of baptism off our backs and onto the backs of the persons being baptized because we doubt that we have the ability to be God's instruments in the task of "making disciples." We doubt that God could use people like us to convert other people. We tell the person being baptized that it is all up to him or her. We tell the parents of the child being baptized that it is all up to them. This is not only irresponsible but biblically indefensible. It is the *church* which has been entrusted with the task of making disciples. Christianity is not a do-it-yourself, home correspondence course in salvation. My salvation is always a gift, something which is received from God and from God working through God's people.

This is not to deny my free will to act or to reject the claim that is made upon me by God in baptism. God's first action in my behalf necessitates my response. The chosen must choose. At many points in my life, I must say yes to God's yes to me in baptism. I have the freedom to say no. But the first thing that happens, the first word which baptism speaks over me, is a loud and clear divine yes. Of course, not everyone who is called puts his or her hand to the plow. But even when I do put my hand to the plow, when I say yes, when I keep my promises, when I answer to my name and come forward, baptism reminds me that it is only because I have first, from the foundation of the ages, been claimed, chosen, called, washed, named, promised, and loved by others whom God chose to use for his saving work.

But all too many of us are either caught in churches which tell us that salvation is something we must do for ourselves or else caught in self-centered attitudes which delude us into thinking that, while others may be moderately helpful in bringing us into the Kingdom, Christianity is basically something which we do, think, feel, or believe on our own. We like to think we are, "self-made men."

I was in a meeting not long ago where persons gave testimonies about their religious experiences. One man rose and said, "I was a Methodist for thirty-eight years before anybody told me about Jesus." Now what he may have meant to say was, "I was a church member for thirty-eight years before I really experienced my faith and before I really lived it." I can understand such delayed response. But I cannot understand the attitude which I am afraid this man meant to express. I am afraid that he was speaking as if he had just begun to hear the real truth about God. I wanted every person who endured him in all of his years growing up in church school, every preacher who had tried to preach to him, every Christian who had tried to tell him about Jesus, to rise up and ask, "What do you think we were trying to get into your head for those thirty-eight years?" All that time other Christians had tried to tell him and show him who he was. Perhaps they did it poorly, but they tried. It may take some people longer to get it into their heads than others. But whenever one wakes up to his or her identity in Christ, it always comes as a gift—given by God who is the story and by God's people who have told us that story, so that it could become our story. We never cease being dependent upon the baptizers.

The "I Found It" bumper stickers that appeared a couple of years ago were dead wrong. According to the Bible, nobody finds God. We may be looking for God, but we usually look in all the wrong places. Most of the time we are looking for ways to *avoid* God! But the gospel story is that God—in God's infinite love and mercy—found *us!* "I Got Found" would be a more biblical way of speaking about our salvation.

It is not quite inaccurate to speak of baptism, particularly infant baptism as "dedication of the child to God." The profound and beautiful truth of baptism is not so much that we *give* our children to God—God *takes them* demanding that "the little children come to me." In baptism, we have been taken by God. We are the chosen.

This is also why "rebaptism" is impossible. If baptism is a purely human sign for something which we do—our decision, our promise, our commitment, our understanding—then I suppose that baptism could be continually repeated since God knows we are forever falling away from our decisions, breaking our promises, changing our commitments, shifting our understandings. On the other hand, if, as classical Christian theology has maintained, baptism is an act of God through the church and if God never falls away, never breaks his promises, never misunderstands who we are, then God's actions in baptism need not be repeated.

Baptism is a public declaration of the promise of God: I will be your God. I will choose you. I will never let you go. I will bring you home.

God always keeps his promises. To "rebaptize" would be saying, in effect: God lied; God did not choose me; God did not bring me home.

This, we do not wish to say.

Most people who request "rebaptism" do so from an inadequate understanding of their baptism. They have been told that baptism is something they or their parents have done and promised. The whole burden of the thing has been put on their shoulders. And it is an almost unbearable burden at times. So they come back to the church asking to be rebaptized because they have not kept their promises, have not maintained good feelings, and have changed their minds time and again. They want to be "rebaptized" in hopes that this time it will "take." The message of the church to these people should be a firm word of encouragement to relax and let God do the mysterious and wonderful work which God began in them at their baptism. That work may take time. It has many peaks and valleys. Sometimes I feel that work in me, and sometimes I do not. Sometimes I understand it, and sometimes I do not. But it is *God's* work, not mine. Once again, baptism should remind me I am always the recipient of that work, not the initiator or first cause. I can relax and enjoy that work because God keeps his promises. God remains faithful to his choices even when I am unfaithful.

I do not always feel like a child of God. I do not always look like a child of God. God knows I do not always act like a child of God! But I am. I am one of God's children not because of what I did or because of who I am but because God chose me, out of all the universe, to be his child. I am owned. When I am anxious or alone or defeated, baptism ought to speak a firm word of comfort to me: "Relax, be calm. You did not choose me, I chose you."

IV

In the earliest baptismal liturgies, after the person had been baptized, he or she appeared before the bishop who embraced the new Christian and then did something of great significance: The bishop dipped his finger into oil and made the sign of the cross on the new Christian's forehead. This was known as the *signation*. The sign of the cross upon a person's forehead was like a brand to show ownership. As sheep are marked to show ownership, so Christians are marked, by baptism, to show who owns them and to what flock they belong. Christians are branded to show who chose them and who owns them.

In Ezekiel's vision (9:4) the Hebrew letter *taw* was put on the foreheads of people who were penitent so that they might be spared in the slaughter of the guilty. Early Christians saw this as a foreshadowing of their practice of signing the foreheads of new Christians. In Revelation (7:3), as plagues and judgments are rendered upon the wicked, destruction is halted until "we have sealed the servants of our God upon their foreheads." A seal on the forehead is a sign of God's favor, ownership, and protection.

Can you now see why we speak of baptism and its sign as a *comfort?* For so long now we have spoken of salvation as work which we must do, some achievement which we must earn. We have told our young to go out and find who they are. We have removed assurance from our old, telling them all the things they must do *if* God is to claim them, love them, and choose them. We have made the Christian life contingent on human works, human goodness, human response, and human belief. Baptism reminds us that we are who we are as a divine gift—not as a human achievement. Our identity is a given. Young and old, we are those who have been chosen by God. That choice determines everything else. We are not homeless orphans who are desperately trying to get into God's good graces. We are royalty who have already received that grace in baptism, and now we, the chosen ones, simply try to live in the light of the grace and gift. The people who say that religion is simply a matter of all of us "trying to get to the same place" are mistaken. The Christian faith is a lifelong celebration, beginning at baptism, of the truth that, by God's grace, we have already arrived!

That mischievous little lad who defiantly announced to his would-be tormentor, "I have been baptized," knew a deep truth all Christians should know: the assurance that no matter how high we rise in this life nor how low we may sink, no matter how we feel or act or think, the most important fact of our lives is that we are the chosen—the elect, the claimed, the adopted, the owned.

Luther reflected upon baptism as sign of God's ownership of us. God has paid a price for us, marked us, bought us. Therefore we can live our lives in the quiet confidence of those who need not fear. We need not fear, reasoned Luther, because the Bible tells us, early on, that God is a "jealous God." God does not take kindly to other gods fooling around with what God owns. And, in baptism, God owns *me!* As the *Heidelberg Catechism* (1563) asked, "What is your only comfort, in life and in death?" Answer: "That I belong—body and soul, in life and in death—not to myself but to my faithful Savior, Jesus Christ."

Paul told the struggling chosen ones in the church at Rome:

You have received the spirit of sonship. When we cry, "Abba! Father!" it is the Spirit himself bearing witness with our spirit that we are children of God, and if children, then heirs, heirs of God and fellow heirs with Christ (Rom. 8:15-17a).

Touch your forehead, remember your baptism, and do not ever forget it.

Make a poster to hang on your wall to express what you have learned.

---

4. Come On In, the Water's Fine

Name a person whom you would trust to raise your child as a Christian if you should die. Write a letter to this person explaining how you would like him or her to treat your child. Be specific.

For thou didst cast me into the deep, into the heart of the seas, and the flood was round about me. —Jon. 2:3

I

Our four-year-old is taking swimming lessons. It was with a certain amount of parental consternation that we took him to the local YMCA a few weeks ago to enroll him in the beginners' swimming classes. I had tried, on a couple of occasions, to teach him some rudimentary techniques of swimming—but with little success. So we decided to let someone else try to teach him to swim.

I had wondered how much a four-year-old could learn about swimming. But to my surprise, when I enrolled him in his class, his teacher said, "I wish we could have gotten him a little earlier. It's so much easier to teach younger children to swim."

"*Younger* children?" I asked in disbelief.

"Oh, we like to get them before they can walk," she replied.

My next question was to ask her how she went about teaching babies to swim. "We just more or less throw them in, and they already know what to do. It helps to get them as young as possible because little babies still follow their instincts and behave naturally in the water. Don't forget, a baby is in water for nine months before it is born. Also, babies are still very trusting and will allow you to do more with them."

I found that interesting. According to the teacher, babies can be taught to swim for two main reasons: They are still doing what comes naturally, and they are more trusting than older children.

That night I stood by the pool and watched a skillful swimming teacher do what I had been unable to do. She coaxed our little boy into the water, pulling him out until the water was over his head. He protested, but she kept tugging, gently but firmly, until he was out in deep water. Then, as gently but as firmly, she encouraged him to put his head under the water. He was reluctant at first, but her firm hand pressed his little head into the water. He sputtered and sneezed a couple of times, but it was not long until he got the hang of it and was holding his head under water for almost a minute. She let go, and to his delight and our surprise, he floated.

We watched in amazement at his rapid progress. "It just goes to show," I said, "that sometimes kids trust other people more than they trust their parents. Look at how much he has done with that teacher."

But my wife corrected me, "Maybe it shows that sometimes we *parents* are the ones who lack the trust."

I think she was right. As I stood there, watching the teacher coax my little one under the deep water, my heart beat fast, my palms moistened, and I could feel the fear rise quickly within me. I knew then that my problem with the swimming was that I lacked the trust to pull it off. I failed to trust my own ability as a swimming teacher and my son's ability as a swimmer. I mistrusted the water itself. My lack of trust was contagious. He failed to swim because I was unable to coax him, gently but firmly, into the water.

II

Trust. It is something so basic to life. Erik Erikson believes that trust is developed within the first few weeks of life. He sees trust as a by-product of the relationship between mother and child. During his or her first weeks of life, a child learns that the world is a trustworthy or untrustworthy place. A child goes to sleep at night. It wakes up in the morning and cries out. Will anyone be there? Will I be abandoned? Will anyone hear my cry and come? The door opens. Mother enters. Mother and baby go through their special little ritual of meeting: the cooing, tickling, kissing, and caressing with which they have come to greet one another every morning. Erikson believes that these predictable, patterned rituals of meeting are crucial in a child's development. They remind the child that somebody cares, that help is always available, that the world is a place to be trusted rather than a place to be feared. Conversely, Erikson believes that if a child fails to experience these rituals of meeting and greeting, a child learns that the world is uncaring and undependable, a learning which can have tragic consequences in later life.

But I would like to add to Erikson's view of trust by observing that trust in children is developed not only by being there at the right time but also by *letting go at the right time*.

The loving parent knows not only when to meet and hold on but also when to depart and let go. Some of us cling to our children in unhealthy, stifling, overprotective ways. What may at first glance look like firm parental love may turn out to be an abuse of parental love in which the parent possesses and binds the child so that the child is unable to grow and develop on its own. Sometimes I think we parents cling to, possess, and overprotect our children out of our own lack of trust in them, ourselves, our world—even our God. It takes a loving, trusting parent to know when to let go, when to coax a child to cast off, when to let the child venture forth into the deep waters of life. This, I think, becomes the supreme test of parental love.

III

When parents bring their children to the waters of the baptismal font, they are present at the right place, at the right time. Here, in the church, at the beginning, they are acknowledging this child as a child of God. They stand before the door of the community, which has been told by its Master, "Whoever receives one such child in my name receives me" (Mark 9:37a).

This is the right time for greeting this little one as a brother or sister in Christ, as cherished by Christ all the more because of its very smallness, as claimed by Christ as his own. The church is the family which is commanded to continue Christ's care of the "little ones," to give them an honored place in our midst. "Only 'little ones'—the poor, the helpless, the oppressed, the young, the old, the outcast 'little ones'—inhabit my Kingdom," he said.

But while the baptism of a child is a time for a ritual of meeting and greeting, baptism is also—in a way that both parents and the church may not fully appreciate—*a time for letting go*.

Parental love, in mothers, in fathers, or in holy mother church, is love which loves so that it can let go. Whenever the love of parents becomes possessive, grasping, tight-fisted love, it is perverted parental love. As a parent I must "train up my child in the way that he should go." But at the end of that training is the inevitable departure. Before that departure, I must use all the means at my disposal to be sure that my child acquires the knowledge and the skills which are needed to function in an adult world. This includes the knowledge and skills which are required for living as a Christian adult.

In the past few years, I have met a number of parents who have gotten the notion that, while parents should train their children in academic and vocational skills, they should not "impose" ethical or religious values upon their children.

"We simply tell our children what we believe, but we also tell them that they are free to make up their own minds," some of these people will say. There was also the father who told me, when I asked why his twelve-year-old son was not in church one Sunday, "Well, he doesn't seem to care too much for church, and, after all, you can't force him to go. Can you?" This same father, I noted, had no problems with forcing his child to go to baseball practice, junior high school, piano lessons, and Boy Scouts. I assume that he "imposes" these activities upon his son because he, as a parent, is sincerely convinced that participation will make for a richer and more satisfying life for his son in the future. Why not feel the same way about the church?

Of course, we have all seen the victims of the parental approach which forced children into patterns of belief and behavior which were unrealistic for the child's needs and abilities. We all know that, in spite of a parent's best efforts, a child may not follow a parentally chosen path. But there is a marked difference between saying, "This is our faith, our family's faith, and the faith that we have promised to give to you, and therefore we want you to participate in this faith"; and saying, "As far as your faith is concerned, that's a matter we completely leave up to you. We have nothing to pass on to you, no experience of our own to share with you, no vision for your future."

One reason that parents may have to force their children to go to church is that the children sense that their parents, in their own adult lives, are uncommitted to the faith which they attempt to force upon their children. It undoubtedly strikes our children as nothing less than hypocrisy for us to attempt to force them down a path we ourselves are unwilling to travel.

My wife and I seriously discussed delaying the baptism of our children until they were old enough to decide about baptism for themselves. But we decided that this would be less than honest about our own expectations and commitments for them. Even though our children, when they grow up, would be as free as any other adults to decide for themselves about their own belief and behavior, while they were under our care, we intended to do our very best to live our lives before them in such a way that they might see the faith in us. Certain options would be unavailable to them because they were our children. While we do not mean to "impose" unrealistic or unnatural expectations upon them, neither do we mean to be dishonest with them about who we are and under what commitments we have chosen to live our lives. We intend to live our lives in such a way as to say, "This is who we are and are trying to be. Therefore, this is who you are. This is our family's way of doing things. This is the witness to the truth which we have received and which we now, with God's help, pass on to you."

I believe that many of us parents suffer from a failure of nerve in regard to the nurturing of our children's faith. We are certain that we will send them to school because we are confident in the value of education. We are certain that they will take piano lessons because we are sure that art enriches a person's life. We insist that they do household chores because we know that the ability to work is basic to adult happiness. But we lack confidence that in matters of religion we have anything special to offer them. We are going through a period in which everything is up for grabs, in which all values are being questioned and many are being jettisoned. So who am I to pass on to my young who they are and what they should be? In other words, we suffer, as parents, not so much from a lack of know-how but from a lack of faith in ourselves, our values, our tradition, our own witness. We suffer from a lack of trust.

But even though this may be true, as a parent I must never forget that all my faithful attempts to train and nurture my child into the faith do not relieve me from the faithful attempt to let go.

47

It is easier to let my child go if I am sure that I have done my best, while the child is under my care, to nurture the child into faith. At any rate, there comes that day, or that score of days, when I must let go: she walks out the door for her first day of school; he tells, me "Thanks, Daddy, but I'd rather do it myself"; she tells you that she will not be the doctor you had hoped she would be; he brings home the girl you did not choose to be his wife. And you let them go, because they must do it themselves or not at all. We would, if we could, shield them from the blows of life. And we would like to save them the heartache of all the mistakes we made as we grew up. But we cannot. They will only learn by making the journey themselves—and there are few shortcuts.

IV

Baptism says this: In matters of faith, you can give them a few ground rules, you can tell them how you felt when you were first plunged under the waters, but they must sink or swim on their own. You can answer for them now, but you cannot believe on their behalf. God has no grandchildren. Each generation must find and be found by God on its own.

You know that the going gets rough. You have already learned what poor Jonah was talking about when he said:

> For thou didst cast me into the deep,
> into the heart of the seas,
> and the flood was round about me;
> all thy waves and thy billows passed over me (Jon. 2:3).

You know that life is not always a walk beside the still waters but can also be a swirling, churning cataract in which "deep calls to deep" (Psalm 42:7) and the waves knock us down and the churning vortex might suck us under and overwhelm us with its surging fury. You love them, and it breaks your heart to see them test the waters with their little toes, because you know the flood may not be far behind. And you would do it for them, if you could, but you cannot. So you let them go. And that letting go is, in itself, an act of the highest faithfulness.

Sometimes we must let them go into the arms of others who can do a better job than we parents of coaxing them into the waters—

48

teachers, guides, pastors, friends. We do this because sometimes, as in swimming, others can push them where you would only seek to protect them. That is why the church, at a child's baptism, reminds the whole church that we *all* assume responsibility for a baptized child. At every baptism, a child ought to be spoken for by an adult sponsor from the congregation. This sponsor can represent the rest of us in saying to the child's parents, "Guiding and nurturing this child of God is too tough and too important a job for you to do on your own, so we'll all do it with you."

Sometimes you simply let them go into the everlasting arms of God himself, the same way you let them go at the font at baptism. You let them go in faith that those same divine arms which claimed your child in baptism will now save your child in adulthood.

Not too long ago a couple asked me, as their pastor, to talk to their rebellious teenager. The boy had gotten into trouble with the law. He had repeatedly run away from home, and his parents were ready to give up on him. I talked to the troubled boy. I told him that we loved him, cared for him, believed in him, and wanted to help him. I wish I could tell you that my conversation turned his life around. But it did not. He listened impassively, thanked me, then walked out. When he walked out, as he was heading out the front door and down the sidewalk, I thought, We are letting you go. Not letting you go to nowhere. We let you go in trust that the God who claimed you and named you in baptism will keep his promise to bring you home. We let you go—to God. Like Cain, wandering in the Land of Nod, this boy has a mark upon him, a sign upon his forehead that shows to whom he belongs. It is the sign of the cross. Sometimes, what applies to our human parents also applies to holy mother church. She has to let her children go, let them wander away to the Land of Nod, east of Eden, in order that they may arrive where she wishes they might have remained all along.

And so, when parents bring their child to the waters of the baptismal font, they do what parents must be doing every day of their child's life—letting go. This is why baptism is not only a joyful occasion but also one which is shot through with pain. Parents stand there, before God and the church, saying to their child, "If we could, we would do your dying and rising for you.

49

We would protect you from the birth pains of all the rebirths you have yet to go through. We would calm the waters and still the seas for you—if we could. But we cannot. So we let go. We let go so that God has room to come. We give you up to God's grace, trusting that God's grace is sufficient, that God will keep the promises which he makes to you in your baptism.''

As Jonah sang, when he was pulled from the depth,

I went down . . . yet thou didst bring up my life from the Pit,
   O Lord my God.
When my soul fainted within me, I remembered the Lord;
   and my prayer came to thee, . . .
   Deliverance belongs to the Lord! (Jon. 2:6-7,9*b*).

And the precious child enters the waters, the child sputters and sneezes, his head goes under, the waters cover him, he bobs back up, he floats, he breathes, he swims, and for the thousandth time one of God's children ventures forth into the deep, sustained by everlasting arms.

Pick out a favorite hymn tune. Write words for that hymn on the topic of Christian child rearing, to be sung at a baptism.

---

5. The Cleansing Bath

Define sin. State as clearly as you can the relationship between sin and baptism.

But you were washed, you were sanctified, you were justified in the name of the Lord Jesus Christ and in the Spirit of our God.—1 Cor. 6:11

I

Bill Muehl, who taught me preaching at Yale, reminded me of a marvelous song from *West Side Story,* "Gee, Officer Krupke." It is sung by a group of young street hoodlums, and it has much to say to our contemporary religious situation.

The boys have been the unwilling beneficiaries of a host of social scientists who have analyzed their criminal tendencies and then blamed their behavior on some condition within society. Sociologists say that the boys are the victims of an oppressive society. Economists say the boys behave poorly because of chronic unemployment. Psychologists dismiss their criminality as the result of adolescent insecurity brought on by insufficient father images. In other words, experts and therapists have assured the boys that they are not responsible for their way of life. They are basically good boys who have been warped by bad circumstances.

Officer Krupke is the cop on the beat whose answer to the boys' problems is a crack on their heads with his club. But Krupke is frustrated by the well-meaning social worker who tells Krupke that what these boys need is sympathy and understanding rather than rebuke and punishment. In the song, "Gee, Officer Krupke," the boys make fun of their benefactors, mimicking those who try to rationalize and excuse their misconduct. The song ends with a joyous chorus in which the boys let everyone know just how Officer Krupke feels about them. They know, that he knows, they are not just misunderstood because really deep down they are all no good.

51

William Muehl notes in his book *All the Damned Angels* that the boys "will not be explained away as social mistakes." They know that they are more than the mere recipients of a corrupt society's corruption. They have a hand in their own corruption. In short, they *sin*. And, in this song, the boys warn all their would-be benefactors that the benefactors are doing them no favor in explaining away their behavior. To take their sin away, their freedom to choose and to do the wrong, is to take away an important part of their humanity: "The best of us is no good."

A few years ago, Karl Menninger's bestseller was titled and asked the question, *Whatever Became of Sin?* He chided those therapists and social scientists who sought to rationalize away all aberrant human behavior as the result of unfavorable social conditions. But Menninger reserved his harshest rebuke for the liberal religious establishment who, for the past few decades, has been telling people, in effect, there is no such thing as sin. For some time now, many people have gotten the impression that "sin" is an unduly judgmental term which has no place within an "I'm OK, you're OK" progressive world view. What was once called "sin" is now dismissed as "alternate lifestyle," "social maladjustment," "failure to live up to one's full human potential," or behavior which is "the result of inadequate education." That ultimate authority by which all human behavior was once judged (God) has been reduced, in the minds of many, to a kindly, all-affirming, all-accepting indulgent therapist who blesses everything and damns nothing.

"Hogwash," said Menninger, in effect. There are, in our world, infidelity, cruelty, racism, stealing, prejudice, lying, idolatry, and a host of other human behavior which can only be called *sin*. Much of this behavior is not a matter for the secular authorities or for secular therapists. But it is a matter for a faith which believes in God. The law of the land is concerned solely with just relationships among citizens. The law of God, however one perceives that God and that law, is concerned with the demands and requirements of God. Failure to live by those demands and requirements may not be a problem for the state. Failure to live by God's demands is only a problem for Christians. That problem can only be called *sin*.

But the average person today seems not overburdened by sin.

We read with curiosity the accounts of people like Augustine, Martin Luther, John Wesley and wonder how thinking people like these could have been so tortured and tormented by something called sin. Perhaps their consciousness of sin was simply part of their pre-scientific world view. Perhaps we have now learned that humanity is basically good, not basically bad, and that the bad behavior of people in this world is attributable to a basically bad world rather than to basically bad people. And yet, can we be let off the hook so easily? The generation who lived through the horrors of World War II—the concentration camps, the bombings, the carnage and destruction, the murder of six million Jews—can this generation now attribute all this to basically nice people who went wrong? Vietnam, racial segregation, the widespread child abuse, rape, soaring divorce rate, or the myriad of everyday, mundane little cruelties and injustices which we inflict on others—is this all simply the mistake of basically good people making wrong choices? A former president appears on television and justifies his behavior in betraying his office as simply, "I made a few errors in judgment." None dare call it sin.

In his book *He Sent Leanness,* David Head offers this tongue-in-cheek rewriting of the Prayer of General Confession from the old *Book of Common Prayer.* Here is the confession which best suits our current ideas about sin and forgiveness:

> Benevolent and easy-going Father: we have occasionally been guilty of errors of judgment. We have lived under the deprivations of heredity and the disadvantages of environment. We have sometimes failed to act in accordance with common sense. We have done the best we could in the circumstances; and have been careful not to ignore the common standards of decency; and we are glad to think that we are fairly normal. Do thou, O Lord, deal lightly with our infrequent lapses. Be thy own sweet Self with those who admit they are not perfect; According to the unlimited tolerances which we have a right to expect from thee. And grant us as indulgent Parent that we may hereafter continue to live a harmless and happy life and keep our self-respect. Amen. (p. 19).

In a recent discussion in an adult church school class, one of the participants offered a definition of *sin* as, "Doing something you know you're not supposed to do." In other words, if you do not know it is wrong to steal, if you have always been taught that it is right to steal, then stealing is not really sinful. Sin, under this definition, is mainly a matter of ignorance, a failure to receive proper education. And yet, in the past decade, we Americans have engaged in a massive effort to provide good education for our citizens. More people are receiving more education than ever. But who can say that we are better than ever? Our acquisition of knowledge simply provides us ever more elaborate ways to explain away, rationalize, and justify our sin.

In the light of all this, it is amazing that some can still argue, before an agreeing audience, that sin and our sinfulness are things which we have now risen above, or, if what was once called "sinful" behavior still persists, it is mainly a matter of inadequate education or insufficient information, a matter which may be rectified by some new government program for social enlightenment. But is it so amazing that we should react in this way? Is not our reaction, our rationalization, our justification, our explaining away of sin the most conclusive evidence for the continuing power of our sin?

Perhaps modern humanity's greatest problem is thinking that it has no problem. As C. S. Lewis said somewhere, the chief evidence that we are indeed "miserable offenders" is that we miserably fail to recognize or admit that we are miserable offenders! The people who party and make merry on the top floor of a skyscraper, while an undiscovered fire makes its way up the floors from the basement, do not know that they have a problem. They may feel, in their merriment, that they have no problems. Yet, in fact, they have a very pressing problem. They are more miserable than they know and that is their chief misery.

Our sin is so deep, so unconquerable by our own efforts, that only the most drastic of actions can make us aware of its presence among us or root it out. Our problem is not just *sins* but *Sin,* with a capital *S*. Our problem is that we are fundamentally disposed to approach all of life selfishly, egotistically, ignorantly, idolatrously. More tragic for the conscientious ones among us, even as we act out of selfishness and self-centeredness, we genuinely think we are acting out of selflessness. We even may call our greatest sinfulness our greatest righteousness. Paul spoke for all earnest seekers of righteousness when he lamented:

I do not understand my own actions. For I do not do what I want, but I do the very thing I hate. Now if I do what I do not want, . . . So then it is no longer I that do it, but sin which dwells within me. . . . I can will what is right, but I cannot do it. For I do not do the good I want, but the evil I do not want is what I do. Now if I do what I do not want, it is no longer I that do it, but sin which dwells within me (Rom. 7:15-20).

Therein lies our human predicament. We do not know what to do; and, when we know, we do not have the will to do it. The modern world may give us an ample stock of rationalizations for this situation. Modern consciences may be so malleable as to make us appear not so bad after all. But, in our fleeting moments of honesty, we know this, too, is part of our sin.

Who can describe such entrapment as anything less than sin? Our problem is not that we have a few minor flaws which need to be modified. Our problem is not that we occasionally slip up and do something we know we should not do. Our problem is that we are fundamentally, culturally, predisposed toward the wrong. Our mistakes, cruelties, lies, conceits, prejudices, infidelities—our sins—are not our main problem, they are the results of our main problem: our Sin. Our *sins* are the end result of our Sinfulness.

We have not talked much about Sin lately. We assume that we are basically nice people who are making progress. But our day-to-day experience of ourselves, the hard facts of modern history, the failures of even our best intentions suggest otherwise. Sin abounds.

II

Baptism addresses itself to our situation in sin. Baptism appears first in the New Testament as a cleansing bath which deals with sin. John the Baptizer opens the Jesus story with a simple sermon: "Get washed up and clean because Messiah is coming." John appears "in the wilderness, preaching a baptism of repentance for the forgiveness of sins" (Mark 1:4).

This "baptism" which John does in the Jordan is not some new or strange religious practice. Throughout the Old Testament, there were various ceremonial washings as signs of the holiness which God required of his people (Lev. 11:45; 12—16, Exod. 29:4, Num. 8:5-7). The God of Israel is not to be worshipped except with "clean hands and a pure heart" (Psalm 24:4). "Wash me thoroughly from my iniquity, and cleanse me from my sin! . . . Purge me with hyssop, and I shall be clean; wash me, and I shall be whiter than snow," pleads the psalmist (51:2, 7).

The cleansing water was not limited to individuals. The whole nation of Israel could be sprinkled clean:

> I will take you from the nations, and gather you from all the countries, and bring you into your own land. I will sprinkle clean water upon you, and you shall be clean. . . . A new heart I will give you, and a new spirit I will put within you (Ezek. 36:24-26).

Eventually, the prophetic vision expanded even beyond the Chosen People. Zechariah prophesies that at the coming Day of the Lord the cleansing waters will be for all nations:

> On that day living waters shall flow out from Jerusalem, half of them to the eastern sea and half of them to the western sea; it shall continue in summer as in winter. And the Lord will become king over all the earth (Zech. 14:8-9).

By the time of Jesus and John the Baptist, the Dead Sea scrolls tell us that frequent ritual baths were practiced by some ascetic communities. These baths were not only ceremonial washings but also involved penitence and submission to God's will. They were seen as final preparation for the dawning of the New Age when the Messiah would come.

Shortly after the time of Jesus, Judaism practiced proselyte baptism of Gentile converts. Proselytes were required to bathe in order to purify themselves before circumcision. Baptism was part of the initiation process into Judaism the same way that it had become the major initiating rite into Christianity. One could not enter a new way of life without first being cleansed of the vestiges of the old life.

The Gospels open with John the Baptist, a strange prophet in the wilderness, commanding people to come to the Jordan and get washed and ready for the Messiah. One prepares for the Messiah by repenting and getting one's sins washed away. Not only must one be washed, one must also "bear fruits that befit repentance" (Luke 3:8). One's life must be changed, turned around, and one's deeds must demonstrate that change. "Even now the ax is laid to the root of the trees," John warns. "Every tree therefore that does not bear good fruit is cut down and thrown into the fire" (Luke 3:9).

When Jesus is baptized by John, John's baptism takes on new meaning. I have spoken and will speak in this book of many of those specifically Christian meanings which Jesus brings to John's water-bath baptism. But none of these new meanings negates the fundamental meaning of baptism as cleansing from sin.

"You were washed," Paul reminds the contentious Corinthians, thereby "you were sanctified, you were justified" (1 Cor. 6:11). Ananias urges Saul to "rise and be baptized, and wash away your sins, calling on his name" (Acts 22:16). Baptism sets our feet on a different path, gives us our true vocation, lets us see our true nature which our sin has obscured. We fall out of the ranks of the enslaved and start marching to the beat of a different drummer.

Aidan Kavanagh reminds us, in his book *The Shape of Christian Initiation,* that baptism is not simply washing, it is *bathing.* One washes clothes or dishes, but one bathes oneself. In the ancient world, the bath was both a personal and social ritual. Bathing was much more than an act of personal hygiene. The magnificent ruins of the Roman baths attest to this. In the bath, one was not only cleansed—one was *changed.*

The receiving of the Spirit is likened to the bath after birth in John 3:3-5 and Titus 3:5-7. Paul compares baptism to a funeral bath and burial in Romans 6:1-11 (see chapter 9), and to a bride's nuptial bath in Ephesians 5:26. The church is the newly bathed bride—refreshed, renewed, adorned, and regenerated for her Christ. Baptism is the bath that plunges one into the "name of Jesus" (1 Cor. 1:13) so deeply that Christians are as set apart by baptism, as Jews before them were set apart by circumcision (Col. 2:1), arraying them in him (Gal. 3:27), burying them in him (Rom. 6:1-11). So radical and complete is this primal experience of baptism that only the most primal of human experiences can convey its meaning: marriage, birth, death, and bathing.

The bath of baptism ended, as did other baths in the ancient world, by anointing with oil—the ancient counterpart of our soap. The body was then arrayed in new or special clothing. "As many

Baptismal font at Cawston
15th century

of you as were baptized into Christ have put on Christ'' (Gal. 3:27). The clothing demonstrated the completely new, fresh nature of the person who had been cleansed in baptism. One emerged from the waters not only cleansed but also *changed*.

III

But there cannot be change in those who think they need no changing. If we suppose that our hands are clean, we have no need to wash. As Jesus said, the whole have no need of a physician. And behind Jesus' words is the implication that the sickest ones of all are those who know not how sick they really are.

Baptism says my sole precondition for authentic conversion into the faith is real sin. The sole requirement for the cleansing bath is real uncleanness. But, oh, how we struggle against that truth! It always seems more reasonable to believe that God is merciful to those who meet certain prior expectations: right ideas, right behavior, right feelings, or, for that matter, right sex or race. ''But when we were right,'' Luther once noted, ''God laughed at us in our rightness.''

God's quarrel is with all of humanity—not merely with certain segments of it. God's wrath falls upon the religious and the non-religious among us. Even the best of our good deeds fail to equal God's goodness. Even our noblest ideas and beliefs do not earn us salvation. ''My ways are not your ways,'' thunders forth the Holy One, devastating our puny, pious pretentions. The good that we would do, none of us has done. We are not right. We sin.

So someone asks, ''If baptism deals with sin, then why do we baptize sweet little babies?'' Once again, if sin is some conscious mistake we have made, some accidental moral indiscretion, then obviously babies do not sin. We should wait to baptize them until they consciously do wrongs and know better. But, if sin is a fundamental, innate, inborn part of the human condition, then sin is part of us from birth. ''Original sin,'' they once called it. Besides, if you do not think babies are basically as self-centered, selfish, and egotistical as the rest of us, you need to be around more babies! Sin comes part and parcel with being human. I am born organizing the whole world around myself. The later myriad of big and little *sins* are only the results of this originating *Sin*.

This inborn Sin is not only individual but also social. We Protestants have been wrong in our almost exclusive focus upon individual sins—the drinking, smoking, cursing sins—and neglect of the social, group sins—the racism, nationalism, sexism sins. In the next chapter we will speak of our salvation as a corporate experience. Our Sin is also a corporate thing. Sometimes the group sins can be more subtle and insidious than the individual sins. In fact, part of our fixation with the personal sins and denial of our social sins are more evidence of our *Sin*. But who is to say which comes first, the individual or the group sins? They go together in most of our lives, feed on one another, depend on one another to warp God's image in us.

That divine image is restored, renewed, discovered again in baptism. We emerge from the baptismal waters as new creations. Never totally new, of course. No matter how dramatic the change, how deep the repentance, how thorough-going the bath, we will continue to have some more repenting to do, some more letting go and letting God do his work in us. As Horace Bushnell said to parents in his day, "Don't think you've done corrupting them when they are born." Individual and social sin continues to act upon our lives even after baptism. Our sin is so entrenched within us, even the best of us, that only a lifetime of change will root it out.

But, admitting all this, let us also admit that God begins that change decisively, radically in baptism. The rest is only the secondary mopping-up action which follows the decisive victory. "Sin no longer has power over us," Paul would say. To those who unduly worried themselves about their sin, John Calvin urged them to draw comfort from their baptism by remembering its cleansing power:

> At whatever time we are baptized, we are once for all washed and purified for our whole life. Therefore, as often as we fall away, we must call up the remembrance of our baptism, so as to feel certain and secure of the remission of our sins. (*Institutes of the Christian Religion,* Book IV, XV, 3.)

In fact, for both Luther and Calvin, the medieval practice of penance could be disregarded because they viewed baptism as the only valid means of dealing with our sins. In the midst of our everyday continuing *sins,* we should remember that baptism has washed our *Sin* and take comfort. This is repentance. Not that we do not continue to be and do wrong. We still sin. But, as Paul said, we no longer live by Sin, hide from it, attempt to explain it away. We can afford to be so pessimistic about human nature because we are so optimistic about God's grace in restoring our rightful vocation. Sin no longer determines us. We come out of the waters as new creatures. Our cleansed lives are given back to us, fresh and new, ready to be begun again. We are no longer anxious and afraid. We can breathe. *We are free.*

IV

My colleague, John Bergland first told me about the baptismal font at Belmont Abbey College in North Carolina. It is made from a huge stone which has been hollowed out for a font. On that very stone, a little over a hundred years ago, black slaves stood to be sold to the highest bidder. Today, the stone serves Belmont Abbey as its baptismal font. An inscription on the plaque tells all who enter those cleansing waters: "On this stone men were sold into slavery. From this stone men are now baptized into freedom."

Write a short story exploring sin and forgiveness to an elementary school child.

61

6. All in the Family

Answer the following questions:
What is the church?
Who is a member of the church?
How does one become a member?

While we were yet helpless, at the right time Christ died for the ungodly.—Rom. 5:6

I

The great heresy of American popular religion is the assertion that "religion is a private affair."

For the past few years, the pollsters have been telling us that, contrary to what many might think, Americans are "religious." More than 90 percent of the Americans polled say they believe in God. But only about half of those polled say they are active in any organized religious group. As George Gallop observed recently, "Americans are more religious than ever. They just don't care much for churches and religious organizations. They're believers but not joiners."

Granted, Americans may be "religious"—if religion is loosely defined as some vague personal sentiment toward some amorphous divinity. But, while it uncertain what those "believers" who are not "joiners" believe in, it is certain that they do not believe in historic Christianity. The Christian faith is neither a set of lofty ideals and noble propositions, nor is it a system of ethics and guides for behavior. The Christian faith is a corporate endeavor, a way of life together under Christ with his holy ones.

Jesus not only preached, taught, healed, and acted, he formed a community, gathered disciples, brought together the most unlikely of people, made them a family. As Paul said to the faction-ridden church at Corinth, the church is Christ's body, his visible presence here on earth, for better or worse, the only form which he has chosen to take in this world. One cannot claim to be "in

Christ" without being in the "body of Christ." There is no solitary Christian, no way of doing the faith by a home correspondence course in salvation. Nor can you do the faith in the cozy comfort of your living room watching an evangelist do the faith on television. He who does not know the church does not know the church's Lord, and he who does not know the Lord does not know God. And baptism is the door.

Against the heresy of "religion is a private affair" and the blasphemy of the "self-made man," baptism reminds us that from beginning to end, our salvation and therefore our identity are corporate products, corporate *gifts*. Baptism reminds us that our redemption is ecclesial from start to finish, socially structured, a group event.

II

In the New Testament, while baptism is intensely personal and individual, it is also corporate and communal—like the Christian life itself. While individuals are baptized in the New Testament (Acts 8:13, 38; 1 Cor. 1:14), there are also group baptisms (Acts 8:12, 10:48; 1 Cor. 1:16). The significance of baptism is invariably described in terms of the "many." Paul uses only plural pronouns—*we, you, us*—to speak of baptism. The newness of the new life in Christ is evident from the way baptism is reported. In the Old Testament, only individuals received the Spirit. At Pentecost, at the birthday of the church, a new thing happens. "About three thousand" were baptized and received the Holy Spirit (Acts 2:41). Thus begins the "*fellowship* of the Holy Spirit" (2 Cor. 13:14; Phil. 2:1, italics added). For Acts, when the Spirit descends and the crowd is baptized, the proof that their baptism is effective, the validation that their church is *his* church is the climax of the Pentecost story: "And they devoted themselves to the apostles' teaching and fellowship, to the breaking of bread and the prayers" (Acts 2:42).

The church is not the club of the like-minded and the similarly disposed. The church is not the chummy togetherness of people who are socio-economically alike or persons who nurture each other's self-interest in a cozy "support group." The church is held together by something more substantial than benign and insipid theological "pluralism" or innocuous assertions that "it

63

doesn't really matter what we believe as long as we're sincere.'' The church is not what we bring to it or what we make out of it, but rather what *God,* in baptism and through the church, brings and makes out of us.

Paul told the bickering Corinthians, ''For by one Spirit we were all baptized into one body'' (1 Cor. 12:13) and proclaimed to the Ephesians:

> There is one body and one Spirit, just as you were called to the one hope that belongs to your call, one Lord, one faith, one baptism, one God and Father of us all (4:4-6*a*).

The church's unity is a gift—not an achievement. For who could explain how so diverse a people as we could come together, except that our togetherness is *grace?*

To be in the church is to be together in God's family, that strange clan, begotten by ''water and the Word.'' Like any family, one cannot *join* the family of God. One must be *adopted.* Joining the church is not simply a matter of joining a voluntary society of religiously inclined people. We do not join the church so much as we are joined into it. Nobody chooses his or her parents. The parents beget and choose the child. The same can be said for the children of mother church.

From the earliest days, Christians spoke of their salvation in terms of ''adoption.'' Baptism, as initiation into the church and into the name of Christ, was compared to adoption, being made a child, an ''heir'' of God Almighty. ''See what love the Father has given us, that we should be called children of God; and so we are'' (1 John 3:1).

III

Nothing underscores the essential nature of both baptism as adoption and salvation as gift so well as the practice of infant baptism. While the church's earliest baptism was probably adult baptism—since the church's earliest baptisms were *missionary* baptisms of adult converts—the baptism of the children of Christian parents was a widespread practice as early as the third century.

Wherever salvation is conceived of as an individual achievement, the result of human action, decision, or belief, then infant baptism will appear meaningless. Obviously, a baby is not good at doing the right action, deciding for itself, or believing the right belief. Nothing could be more incapable of individual achievement than a little, helpless, dependent baby. A baby must have everything done for it if it is to survive.

But wherever salvation is viewed primarily as a gift, the corporate bestowal of something which cannot be earned, merited, achieved, or bought, then babies may be baptized. The only requirement to receive a gift is to be receptive. The only requirement to be helped is to be helpless. And what is more receptive, helpless, dependent, weak, and needy than a baby? *Precisely*.

Every time the church baptizes a baby, we are saying this baby at age six weeks looks just like you or I look at age six months, six, or sixty years—so far as your relationship to God is concerned. You never cease being dependent upon God and God's church to do for you what you cannot do for yourself. As was stated in chapter three, you do not choose God—God chooses you. You never get so old, so mature, so strong, so self-sufficient, so adept at love that you will not be dependent upon God to love you, adopt you, choose you, and bring you home. As Paul said to those who thought of salvation as the result of human goodness, "While we were yet helpless, at the right time Christ died for the ungodly" (Rom. 5:6).

Paul might as well have said, "While we were still *babies*—helpless, weak, dependent, needy babies—Christ died for us." In the Bible, God always seeks and saves the weak and helpless—only the weak and helpless. The strong and self-sufficient need no savior, so they get none. We baptize babies not because they are better than the rest of us. The only advantage babies have over us adults is that babies may be less confused than we about the limits of their ability to save themselves. Is that why Jesus said that the Kingdom belongs to them?

What could be more weak than a baby, and, therefore, who could be a more fitting object of God's love and our baptism?

The baptism of the children of Christian parents may be justified on two grounds: (1) our belief in the nature of the grace of God; and (2) our belief in the nature of faith by which we receive God's grace.

First, as we have said, new life in Christ is a gift, offered without price to all. Baptism is both means and sign of that gift. It is not a person's understanding of that gift which brings the gift. If it were, then grace would not be grace. What binds God's saving action to baptism is God's doing. This is God's grace and it is offered freely to all. Churches which do not baptize babies often say they wait "until the child is old enough to know what it means" or "until the child is able to decide on his own." But maturity, insight, knowledge, and feelings are never preconditions for salvation. To make a person's understanding or decision a precondition for God's grace is arbitrarily to add something to what the Bible says about grace. It is to make the person's understanding or decision the alternative source of salvation alongside God's grace. What kind of gift is that?

This is not to argue for some kind of mechanistic rite which insures our deliverance. Baptism is not a magical shower upon someone which makes that person a Christian regardless of the person's disposition toward the rite. Not everyone who is called puts his or her hand to the plow. Baptism, in itself, does not insure my "salvation." Rather, baptism insures that my whole life, from birth to death, start to finish, will be under the promise and sign of the cross. Baptism is a sign and means of God's ceaseless striving for us, the ceaseless urging of his grace. God reaches for us first when we are baptized as babies, and God continues to reach for us throughout life. The gift of baptism may be rejected and lost.

We are free not to be who we are created to be. I may answer to some alien name, live under some foreign sign, wander, like the prodigal son, into some "far country," where I attempt to live on my own rather than by God's grace. While this is a real possibility, baptism represents the greater possibility that God's grace, God's ceaseless striving, God's ceaseless urging will finally bring me home. As the old song says, "*Grace* will lead me home." And, in a self-help, "self-made man," achievement-oriented society, grace will always appear to be amazing.

Therefore, to ask whether infants and children may be baptized is to ask whether God's grace and salvation are free enough, undeserved enough, unmerited enough, and great enough to include even children. Every time we baptize a baby, we proclaim to all the world that God's grace is sufficient. And it is given freely to all.

But grace is usually not the problem in our baptism of infants. The usual objection is that, in the Bible, one must have "faith" in order to be baptized. This faith is the prerequisite for baptism. How can advocates of infant baptism live with a statement like Mark 16:16, "He who believes and is baptized will be saved." An infant cannot believe. Then how can an infant be baptized?

Well, it is not as simple a question as it might sound. In the New Testament, faith itself is God's gift and creation, not our achievement. Faith is not a condition or quality which one must have in order to receive God's grace. Faith is not the human contribution to the cost of salvation. The New Testament says, again and again, that the opposite of "faith" is "works" (Rom. 3:27; Gal. 2:16; Titus 3:5-7), and it matters little whether we are talking about works of belief, trust, tithing, feelings, decisions, understanding, or any other human-initiated response.

Faith itself is *God's* gift. Faith happens when I am grasped by God, not when I grope around for God. Where faith is understood as human grasping for God, only adults can be baptized. Where faith is seen as the reception of a gift, infants may be candidates for that gift.

Richard Jungkuntz offers an analogy in *The Gospel of Baptism* which helps us understand the nature of faith as a gift: Faith is like the darkness of a room which is suddenly lighted. The darkness does nothing except to "receive" the light. It contributes nothing. It simply receives. But when the light shines, the room changes dramatically. It becomes a very different room. It is full of light. Without the light, the darkness is simply darkness. With the light, the darkness is transformed. What was once darkness has become, because of the light, itself, enlightened:

> In him was life, and the life was the light of men. The light shines in the darkness, and the darkness has not overcome it . . . . to all who received him, who believed in his name, he gave power to become children of God (John 1:4b,5,12).

Faith is receptive. Its function is to receive—which is not exactly the same as the catchword for modern evangelism, *accept*. Faith comes, not when we *accept* Christ, but as God in Christ *accepts us* and we receive that acceptance. In other words, faith comes to you in the same way that life comes to you—as a gift.

You do nothing to earn that life nor do you do anything to earn the abundant, eternal life. You simply receive it. You live it. Faith is like that.

When this new life is received, death will be overcome, and the new life will be known, felt, understood, and responded to in your life. That is why the New Testament invariably speaks of faith in terms of its fruits: belief, trust, knowledge, obedience, joy, and love. But we must not equate the fruits of faith with faith. These fruits are the result, the concrete evidence of faith.

One more analogy of faith and baptism might be helpful. As was stated earlier, a primary New Testament way of speaking both of salvation and of baptism as the means and symbol of salvation is *adoption*. When parents adopt a baby, the baby does not realize that he or she is being adopted. The baby has no choice in the matter. But when the adoption is completed, that child becomes their child. The baby's status has changed. Later, as the child grows, the baby may accept his status as a child of his parents. Faith is simply the accepting of that status. It is not the child's acceptance that makes him the parents' son or daughter. Likewise, faith does not make us sons and daughters of God. We are God's children because of the saving event which has happened to us in baptism. We may accept that new status (which is faith) or we may reject it (unbelief). Faith is simply the acceptance of our new status. Unbelief is simply the rejection of what God has done.

Let us carry this adoption analogy one step further. Once a child is adopted, how does that parent treat the adopted child if the child is disobedient? Does the parent kick the child out of the family? No. The child's disobedience may put a strain on the parent-child relationship, but the child's waywardness does not end the relationship. Parents continue to love the child, to work for the restoration of the relationship through discipline, love, and long-suffering. Parents are like that.

In baptism, once God has adopted us as his own, God does not kick us out, even when we disobey. God reaches out. God searches until he finds. God heals our brokenness. Once God has called us in our baptism, once we are adopted, God does not let us go easily. My friend Chad Davis said he used to visit in our state penitentiary and watch fathers who had sons in jail come, day

68

after day, and call on their jailed sons, only to be sent away because the sons refused to see them. But the fathers kept returning each day, in spite of their sons' refusals, hoping that someday their sons would receive them.

God is like that—even more so.

IV

The practice of infant baptism suffers today mainly from what I call "promiscuous baptism." While we are free to baptize the children of Christian parents, we are not free to baptize children for whom there appears to be little or no possibility of responsible nurture into the faith. Otherwise we might as well "baptize" people indiscriminately with a garden hose as they walk down the street. But that would be magic, not grace. If there is no one to affirm the faith of God in and for the child, if no one is present who will promise to proclaim the gospel to the growing child, if no one is there to be the instrument of God's grace for the child, then it would be better to postpone baptism until such time that either the parents or the church can be more responsible. But such postponement is more judgment upon the unfaithfulness of the church than upon the unfitness of the child.

Infant baptism is a mockery when it is done outside the context of parents and a church which nurture the child. Baptism is a gift. But we must be instruments of God's gift of grace. Baptism is most effective where there is a community of faith which is capable of the kind of long-term, lifelong conversion and nurture of those who are born in Christ. "Private baptisms" where the church is not present make about as much sense as a birthday party with a guest list of one. You cannot baptize people into isolation. The church's presence and full participation in the rite are not just a nice thing to do. They are the whole point. Fortunately, the new baptismal rites give more opportunities for congregational participation in the baptismal ritual.

The *church* bears the burden and the command to baptize. We are the ones who are to go "make disciples." The baptizers (the church) bear the burden of proclaiming God's love for the world—a blessed burden which calls forth the best we have. What great confidence God has shown in us to give *us* the mandate to "make disciples." We in the church are simply the gifted ones

69

Baptismal font at Ruabon
19th century

who, in turn, give God's gift to others. Baptism not only incorporates us into the church but also reminds the church, again and again, of who she is and what she is supposed to be doing.

In a fundamental sense, baptism is dedication. But it is not "dedication" in the way people often apply that phrase to baptism. At baptism, parents do not so much dedicate their children to God, rather, the parents acknowledge that God has done something for their children. When children are baptized, the *parents* and the *church* are dedicated! We are dedicated as instruments of God's love and grace so that these beloved children might "grow in grace."

All of our Christian education, family devotions, involvement of children in worship, youth ministry, sermons, confirmation classes, altar calls, family night covered dish suppers, weddings, funerals, and Lord's Suppers are part of the church's continuing baptismal work. These are all part of the church's gift. That is why children must be fully included, fully present, full participants in all of the church's life—especially the church's worship life. After all, how did you learn what it meant to be a part of your human family and to bear its name? How did you learn what it meant to support and to be supported by the family? You learned by being given responsibility in the family, by eating at the family's table, by loving and being loved. So too, in the family of God, we grow by participation and experience. Children learn by doing.

The other day I helped a minister baptize two people. One person was a man who was about thirty years old. He had been converted to the faith a short time before and was now being baptized. The other person was a three-month-old baby girl, child of parents who were active in the church.

First the minister baptized the baby. After he baptized her, he took her in his arms and said to her, "Mary, we have baptized you and have received you into the church. God loves you and has great plans for your life. But you will need the rest of us to tell you the Story, and, from time to time, to remind you who you are, and to keep you in God's family. We are going to specially appoint some of our members to guide you and watch over you as you grow in faith. And all of us promise to adopt you as a sister in Christ."

71

Then the minister baptized the man. After he baptized him, he had him stand before the church and said to him, "Tom, we have baptized you and have received you into the church. God loves you and has great plans for your life. But you will need the rest of us to tell you the Story, and, from time to time, to remind you who you are, and to keep you in God's family. We are going to specially appoint some of our members to guide you and watch over you as you grow in faith. And all of us promise to adopt you as a brother in Christ."

The promises of baptism, the burdens placed upon the baptizers, the evangelistic word of grace, the loving action of God, the demand for lifelong response are the same for all—no matter what the age of the one who is baptized. So, at whatever age we enter those graceful waters, we emerge rising from darkness to light, from loneliness to community, as fragile and dependent as a newborn baby, needing the love and warmth of God's human family.

Review your answers and in the light of this chapter rewrite your answers.

---

7. You've Got Spirit

Read Mark 1:1-11. Describe the difference
between the baptism of John and Jesus.

There is one body and one Spirit, . . . one Lord, one faith,
one baptism, one God and Father of us all, who is above
all and through all and in all.—Eph. 4:4-6

I

When I first moved into this neighborhood, my next-door neighbor, upon learning that I was a preacher, promptly introduced herself as being "charismatic." She said she had received the "baptism of the Holy Spirit." I responded by saying, "That makes two of us."

I could tell from her expression that she was skeptical of my claim. A few conversations later, she became downright incredulous of my assertion that I too was "charismatic."

"I'm praying for you," she said one day leaning over the hedge, pointing her hedge clippers at me in a menacing way.

I thanked her and asked if she were praying for anything specific for me. She said she was. "I'm praying that you'll receive the gift of the Holy Spirit."

I thanked her again and told her that she need not bother God with that request since the Lord had quite graciously given me the Spirit already.

I could tell that she doubted. "Really?" she asked. "I would be interested to know how and when you received the Holy Spirit."

"I can tell you that," I responded. "I was a few months old at the time. A preacher named Forrester took me in his arms, poured water on my head, and told me I had the Holy Spirit."

"That isn't baptism of the Holy Spirit," she retorted.

"Well, the preacher said I got it, and everybody else said I got

73

it. And, if that didn't take, when I was about ten years old, another preacher named Herbert stood me up in front of the church, put his hands on my head and said, in effect, 'You've got the Spirit. Now use it.' And, as if that were not enough, a bishop named Tullis put his hands on my head one night in my mid-twenties and said, 'You've got the Spirit, now get out there and preach the gospel.' About the worst you could say for me is that I don't use the Spirit's gifts, or I don't always live by the Spirit, but you sure can't deny that I've got it.''

All of this so thoroughly baffled my ''charismatic'' neighbor that she shook her head in dismay and began furiously clipping her hedge while muttering something to herself about ''dear Lord.''

In this so-called ''Age of the Spirit,'' as the Neo-Pentecostal Movement sweeps through our churches, where the ''gift of tongues'' and other manifestations of the Holy Spirit are often referred to as ''baptism in the Spirit'' or ''second baptism,'' some may wonder what all this has to do with baptism. Such language challenges the church's traditional understanding of baptism. Such language tends to view baptism as only a first chapter in God's dealing with us, a rather insignificant beginning which needs something else, some later contribution by God before we are truly saved.

In this line of reasoning, our first baptism is only ''water baptism,'' which pales into insignificance alongside the later and more powerful ''baptism of the Spirit.'' Infant baptism is thus reduced to an outward, ritual promise of things to come, administered by a church and a minister. ''Baptism of the Spirit,'' on the other hand, becomes a personal experience of the reality of Christ which comes directly from Christ himself. One is a churchly ritual, the other is a life-changing experience.

The result of this kind of thinking about baptism is often a kind of ''me graduate school Christian, you kindergarten Christian'' boasting. Baptism becomes a quaint little rite (often referred to by the misnomer ''christening'') of no consequence for one's salvation, a prelude to the real business of later adult conversion or the later gift of tongues or later confirmation, a cute dedication service for the parents of a child, or a mere statement after the fact of an evangelical conversion experience. Does baptism ''make disciples," giving them the graceful endowments they need to do God's work, or does it not? Am I a Christian by virtue of my baptism or must I yet await some other divine work in me? Does the New Testament speak of two kinds of baptisms? What is the relationship between "water baptism" and "spirit baptism"?[2]

II

The New Testament does speak of *two* baptisms. One, the baptism of John the Baptist, is *pre*-Christian, a baptism of water as a sign of human repentance, human cleansing. The other, the baptism of Jesus, is with water *and* the Spirit as a sign of *God's* presence and activity.

Let us look briefly at the baptism of John the Baptist, because it is often confused with Christian baptism. John is portrayed in the manner of the Old Testament prophets. Isaiah 40 is quoted in describing John as "a voice crying in the wilderness preparing the way of the Lord." John dresses like a prophet and eats like a prophet. He is strange and harsh, full of threats of doom. John is the pre-Christian prophet pointing the way to the one who comes after him.

The message of this *preparer of the way* is a message of repentance. John preaches a "baptism of repentance" for "the forgiveness of sins." Who does the "work" in John's baptism? Those who repent. The people who get washed and ready for the coming Messiah are the active agents in John's ritual sign of human preparedness. This baptism of repentance is only a temporary stage in God's work with his people, according to John. Someone greater than John is coming with a different baptism. John says, "I have baptized you with water, but *he* will baptize you with the Holy Spirit" (Mark 1:8). John's baptism is in order for men and women to get ready. John says that Jesus' baptism, on the other hand, will be a baptism of God's presence. God, not a man, will be the active agent in this promised baptism of the Holy Spirit.

When Jesus appears on the banks of the Jordan and insists that he be baptized by John, something very significant happens in the midst of Jesus' baptism. The action shifts suddenly from an act of man to an act of God. The heavens open, the Spirit descends upon Jesus like a dove. A voice speaks, "Thou art my beloved Son."

Jesus is the sign of the presence of God. God's Spirit rests on him. The Spirit testifies to all the world who Jesus is. His baptism becomes the occasion for that testimony of the Spirit. When John's Gospel reports the event (1:33-34), we are told explicitly that Jesus' baptism is the baptism of the Holy Spirit. The baptism of Jesus is not a ritual of human preparedness, human repentance, human cleansing; because there is now nothing for which to get ready. The Kingdom is here, in the "midst of you," present in Jesus. Jesus' baptism is not by John but by the Holy Spirit.

There are two types of baptism in the New Testament. One is pre-Christian baptism and the other is Christian baptism. It is a mistake to identify John's baptism as "water baptism" and then to confuse it with Christian baptism. This makes "baptism of the Spirit" some kind of later or second Christian baptism. The New Testament says there is but one Christian baptism and it is with water *and* the Spirit.

The phrase "baptism with the Holy Spirit" occurs only one place in the New Testament, Acts 1:15, where the risen Christ tells the disciples to wait in Jerusalem until they shall be "baptized with the Holy Spirit." That promised gift of the Spirit is fulfilled in the Pentecost story of Acts 2. The disciples were filled (baptized) with the Holy Spirit and began to speak in other tongues. Some thought they were drunk. But Peter's explanation of all this strange behavior was simple. In his sermon, Peter tells the wondering crowd that Jesus, having received the promise of the Holy Spirit from his Father, now, in turn, pours out the Spirit on his disciples (Acts 2:32-33).

If that were the end of the story we might well assume that we, like those first disciples, should wait patiently for the reception of the Spirit which manifests itself in speaking in tongues. This is what the Pentecostal churches of this century have preached. But the story of Pentecost ends, not with the strange tongues but in Acts 2:37-39 where the crowd in the street, deeply moved by Peter's sermon, wonders "What must *we* do to be saved?" Peter's response is straightforward: "Repent, and be baptized every one of you in the name of Jesus Christ for the forgiveness of your sins." That sounds like John the Baptist's sermon. But it is not. Peter continues, *"And you shall receive the gift of the Holy Spirit. For the promise is to you and your children"* (Acts 2:38-39, italics added).

76

Peter here says that the Holy Spirit is promised, not just to the first disciples, but to "us and our children," and baptism is the means of accomplishing that promise. We are not to read ourselves back into what happened to the disciples at Pentecost. We are to see ourselves and our children amidst the crowd. We and the crowd must be baptized to be saved and, when we are baptized into the name of Jesus, we are baptized into the Holy Spirit. Whenever the Holy Spirit is mentioned in the rest of the Book of Acts, it is never related to "baptism of the Holy Spirit." Wherever mentioned, the Holy Spirit always stands related to *baptism* "in the name of Jesus."

In that strange story of Apollos in Acts 18 and 19, we are told that Apollos "knew only the baptism of John" (Acts 18:25*a*). The people at Ephesus were baptized by Apollos and therefore had not even heard of the Holy Spirit (Acts 19:2). In the only instance of "re-baptism" in the New Testament, Paul baptizes them "in the name of the Lord Jesus" so that they might *receive the Holy Spirit*. Jesus' baptism is Spirit baptism. There is only one Christian baptism in the New Testament. It is baptism in the name of Jesus, and it is Spirit baptism.

This linking of water and spirit began in the Old Testament. Isaiah could say,

> I will pour water on the thirsty land, and streams on the dry ground; I will pour my Spirit upon your descendants, and my blessing on your offspring (Isa. 44:3).

Peter picks up on Joel's symbol of "pouring out" the Spirit in his Pentecost sermon:

> This is what was spoken by the prophet Joel: "And in the last days it shall be, God declares, that I will pour out My Spirit upon all flesh. . . . And it shall be that whoever calls on the name of the Lord shall be saved" (Acts 2:16, 17*a*, 21).

While baptism and the gift of the Holy Spirit are integrally related, this is not to claim that the Spirit is given *at* baptism, chronologically or mechanistically speaking. In the Book of Acts, the Holy Spirit is bestowed both before baptism (Acts 10:44f) and immediately after baptism (Acts 19:5-6). Sometimes the Spirit is associated with the gesture of laying on of hands after baptism (Acts 8:14ff). In fact, the laying on of hands (an ancient Jewish gesture of commissioning and blessing) was probably more closely associated with the gift of the Spirit than the water bath. But remember that both the bath and the laying on of hands are *baptismal* activities. They are best thought of as parts of the same rite. The separation of the baptismal laying on of hands into a separate rite of "confirmation" (which occurred in the Middle Ages) is an unfortunate development which tends to obscure the integral relationship between the various baptismal acts and tends to disjoin the Spirit from baptism, a disjuncture which, we see from scripture, is unwarranted.

III

But is that all there is to the Christian life? Is baptism both the beginning and the end of our Christian pilgrimage? What about later experiences such as later "gifts of the Spirit" like "speaking in tongues" or even those Wesleyan "heart-warming" conversion experiences? What do these experiences have to do with baptism? Do these later experiences not challenge the meaning and the effectiveness of baptism, particularly infant baptism?

When a person has an adult "heart-warming" conversion experience or experiences the "gift of tongues" or some other experienced, life-changing, dramatic event, baptism, particularly infant baptism, seems to pale into insignificance. After all, how can a non-experiential event like infant baptism (you cannot feel it happening to you) rank in equal importance alongside an experiential event like "being baptized in the Spirit"? How can a non-cognitive event like infant baptism (you do not understand what you are doing) rank in equal importance alongside a cognitive event like adult conversion or an adult "decision for Christ"?

I remind you of what was said about baptism, about salvation, about grace, and about faith in the preceeding chapter. Baptism is *God's* work, not ours. Salvation is God's gift, not our achievement. Grace is a gift. So is faith. In baptism, God adopts us as his own. God reaches for us, grabs for us, claims us as God's chosen ones, as heirs, as royalty. Baptism occurs, not because we have come to God, but because God has first come to us. So, we come. We are baptized. But this baptism is not the end. It is the beginning of a lifelong pilgrimage with God, a lifelong discourse with our Creator. We say now what we have implied before: Baptism is no mere momentary rite. It is a lifelong process of conversion and nurture which begins at the font and does not end until death, until we are at last tucked safely into the everlasting arms of the God who first reached for us in baptism.

And God reaches for us throughout our lives. The "promise to us and our children" at baptism is that the God who first grabbed for us in baptism will not cease dealing with us until he has finished what he began in us at baptism. Baptism is a once-and-for-all event which usually happens when we are babies but takes our whole life to finish.

Every day we must live our baptism. Every day we must respond to God's gracious gifts in our lives. Whether we are baptized at age six months or age sixty years, the day after our baptism we must renew our baptismal vows, open ourselves again to God's work in our lives, say yes in all the big and little things we do and people we meet and promises we keep throughout the day.

A major part of God's daily saving work in our lives is God's gift of God's Spirit. Those who believe that baptism, particularly infant baptism, cannot rate in importance with such experiences as "second (or third or fourth) baptisms" and later conversion experiences, do not realize that baptism is a continuing, daily experience of God's work in us. Daily, God renews in us what he began in our baptism. In our baptism, God has turned to us so that we might turn to him. Daily we turn, responding to what God is doing in us. We respond to the Spirit's urging within our lives. In fact, the response itself (faith) is part of the Spirit's work in us. The new "charismatics" are so right in reminding us that the Spirit is not optional equipment for Christians. It is not a nice extra to have if you can afford it. The Holy Spirit permeates the Christian's existence, begins the Christian's pilgrimage, and leads us daily, tugging at our lives until they be fully turned toward God. There is no conversion, repentance, good work, or good life which is not a gift of the Spirit. And daily it is given freely to all.

Now this is not to deny that on a certain day such an experience of turning (conversion) may be more strong or vivid than on other days. This is not to deny the reality of dramatic, life-changing,

79

soul-shaking conversion experiences which may be accompanied by speaking in tongues, tears, joy, new commitments, changed attitudes, or a host of other gifts. But these are all *gifts*. And, no matter how dramatic or significant the gift, it does not mean there will be no more in store for us the rest of our lives. There is no conversion experience, be it at Aldersgate Street or on the Damascus Road or anywhere else, that means that we will not need to turn to God again for help the next day. We never become too gifted. Daily, we turn.

All of this is to say that later gifts of the Spirit which follow our baptism, later conversion experiences, and later rites of confirmation are best understood as daily experiences or renewals of our baptism. Every day we further penetrate the significance of our baptism for our lives. Every day we discover new gifts which have been given to us through the outpouring of God's love. When we are baptized, at whatever age, we are joined into God's gracious work in the future, and we become the recipients of God's gracious work in the present.

God keeps his promise at baptism. The Spirit is busy in us every day. Some days the Spirit's work in me is especially vivid and meaningful, some days it is not. Some days I respond in faith to the Spirit's leadings, some days I do not respond. But my response or lack of it does not deny its presence in my life. And its presence has been there at least since my baptism. I think of it this way: When I was born, I was given all of my natural endowments. I possessed within my body all the genetic characteristics which I would have for the rest of my life. My hands may be the hands of a great concert pianist. I do not know, because I have never had piano lessons and I have never tried to develop my hands for the piano. Likewise, at my birth at baptism, I have been given all the spiritual endowments which I will ever have. They are mine, not as possessions or achievements but, like my natural endowments, as gifts of God. I have developed, enjoyed, used, and shared some of those gifts. Many have not even been discovered by me yet. And we can thank contemporary "charismatics" and Neo-Pentecostals who have prodded the rest of us into being more responsive to the Spirit's leadings in our lives. I await the time when the circumstances of life or the promptings of the Spirit or the needs of others call forth the Spirit's gifts within me. When they are called forth, that will be a continuing living out of my baptism, a continuing completing of what God began in me at my birth.

So, in a way, we do experience "second baptism." But it may or may not have anything to do with "speaking in tongues," because God's gifts are rich and varied. Every day the God who named us and claimed us and gifted us in baptism claims us again. I must be claimed, again and again and again. And it is all the Spirit's work. There is no blueprint or pattern for that claim upon you or me. One gift is not better than some other gift. You and I have gifts which have been given to us from our birth that we have not stumbled on yet, much less used to their full potential. We have missions to accomplish which we have not yet dared to venture. We do not know where the Spirit will lead us next, or what gifts we have been given, or where God may ask us to use them. All we know is that God knows what he is doing with us. The Spirit blows where it will, and daily it blows through our lives, refreshing us, disrupting us, soothing us, prodding us, and pouring out God's love upon us until we are made over in his likeness.

Baptism tells me what my dull spirit forever wants to forget: As I emerge from the waters, I feel a cool, refreshing breeze about me. That Holy Breath will stick with me through all the dry, dusty summers of my life, a constant friend and comforter who will not leave me be until it has taken me where it will. We are all "charismatic" by virtue of our baptism. We are all *gifted*.

Write a letter to a friend explaining the relationship between baptism and the gift of the Holy Spirit.

81

8. How to Be Born Again

What does the phrase "to be born again" mean to you?

By his great mercy we have been born anew to a living hope. . . . You have been born anew, not of perishable seed but of imperishable, . . . Like newborn babes.
—*1 Pet. 1:3, 23; 2:2*

I

The decade of the seventies may not be remembered, religiously speaking, only as the "Age of the Spirit"; surely someone will also remember us as the "twice born." In his popular book *How to Be Born Again,* Billy Graham speaks of this dramatic, life-changing, heart-felt conversion experience. According to the Gallup poll, "More than one-third of those who are old enough to vote have experienced 'born again' religious conversions" (p. 7). Suddenly it seems as if everybody, from presidents to football players, is reporting born-again experiences.

In *How to Be Born Again,* Billy Graham writes for all those who would like to have this same dramatic, life-changing, transforming experience in their lives. His book is a kind of self-help, do-it-yourself volume on how to get the experience for yourself. By the end of the book, he leads his readers in a simple method of making it happen: (1) "We must recognize what God did." (2) "We must repent for our sins," (3) "We must receive Jesus Christ as Savior and Lord," (4) "We must confess Christ publicly." "Make it happen *now!*" he tells his audience. "If we are willing to repent for our sins and to receive Jesus Christ as our Lord and Savior, we can do it now. At this moment we can either bow our head or get on our knees and say a little prayer." The prayer he suggests for us, if we want to get reborn, goes like this:

O God, I acknowledge that I have sinned against You. I am sorry for my sins. I am willing to turn from my sins. I openly receive and acknowledge Jesus Christ as my Savior. I confess Him as Lord. From this moment on I want to live for Him and serve Him. In Jesus' name. Amen. (pp. 168-169).

Billy Graham's argument is appealing. It is simple, straightforward, understandable, and achievable. He clearly tells us what to do if we want to get born again. But I have two problems with his book and the point of view it represents:

First, we should note that in both the method and the prayer, conversion, salvation, and rebirth are pictured mainly in terms of what we are supposed to do or believe, as a list of four ''musts'' which we must do if we are to be born again. We must recognize, repent, receive, and confess. God's grace is pictured as something good for us, which is out there somewhere and which we must, through a simple four-step method, go out and get for ourselves. It is up to us. Only we can ''make it happen *now!*'' While Billy Graham gives God some credit for being active in leading us into the way of salvation, the help is mostly in the way of setting things clearly before us which we must accept, discover, understand, and do for ourselves.

Such religion is essentially self-help, human conditioned and initiated. That is its fundamental problem. Why would Jesus have spoken of the life he called us to as re*birth,* if that life was mostly a matter of what we decided, did, understood, and discovered for ourselves? After all, how much did we have to do with our first birth? What were the decisions, commitments, and understandings required of us for that first gift of life?

When Jesus told old Nicodemus that ''unless one is born anew, he cannot see the kingdom of God'' (John 3:3), the old sinner was understandably perturbed. ''How can a man be born when he is old?'' Nicodemus asked. We did not pull off our first birth nor can we very well pull off our second—on our own. First or second birth is therefore an impossibility, Nicodemus reasons. That is the whole point. Birth or rebirth *is* impossible for us to do by ourselves. Jesus underscores this with one of his ''with-man-it-is-impossible-but-with-God-all-things-are-possible'' statements. He tells the bewildered old man, ''The wind (the same Greek word for *spirit*) blows where it wills, and you hear the sound of it, but

83

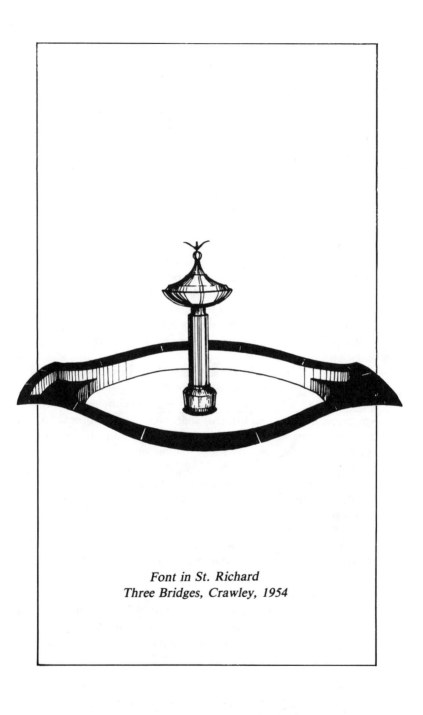

Font in St. Richard
Three Bridges, Crawley, 1954

you do not know whence it comes or whither it goes'' (John 3:8a). In other words, the ''wind,'' the Spirit, is *God's*. God initiates and controls its workings. When we are ''born of water and the Spirit'' (John 3:5), it is part of *God's* work. We do not do it for ourselves—nor can we—because we are talking about something so radical, so new, so dramatic as *birth*. Many Evangelicals today do not give strong enough emphasis to rebirth as God's work, not ours.

Second, and this is related to the first problem, *How to Be Born Again* never once, so far as I could see, mentions baptism. This is strange, not because every book on being a Christian ought to mention baptism (although that is an appropriate place to begin), but because, in the New Testament, any talk about rebirth, regeneration, or being born again is invariably baptismal talk. When the early church heard Jesus talking to Nicodemus about being ''born of water and the Spirit,'' it knew that he was talking about the water and Spirit of baptism—not some vague inner feeling or some four-step method of getting right with God. How does salvation come? Paul is clear: ''He saved us . . . by the *washing of regeneration* and renewal of the Holy Spirit'' (Titus 3:5, italics added).

The best analogy (other than the analogy of burial) Paul could think of for what happened in the baptismal process was human procreation. When Paul thought of the waters of baptism, he thought of the waters of the womb. Life was created from the waters. ''There were heavens and earth long ago, created by God's word out of water and with water'' (2 Pet. 3:5, NEB). Human life is procreated, begins its first nine months, and comes forth from the *waters* of the womb. Birth. So the great baptismal hymn of First Peter sings,

By his great mercy we have been born anew to a living hope. . . .
You have been born anew, not of perishable seed but of imperishable. . . . Like newborn babes (1 Pet. 1:3, 23; 2:2).

We get born, reborn, in baptism.

The rebirth of renewal of which the New Testament speaks is not only a kind or second birth, it is also a *recreation*. Jesus speaks of the ''new world'' which God is bringing forth (Matt. 19:28). The phrase comes from Jewish writing about life after

85

death. The "re" denotes another or a second version of what God has done once before. What is renewed in baptism? Creation. We become a "new creation" as Paul said it:

> Therefore, if any one is in Christ, he is a new creation; the old has passed away, behold, the new has come. All this is from God, who through Christ reconciled us to himself (2 Cor. 5:17-18a).

In other words, our present state is but a broken image of God's original intention for us in creation. But God is not finished with his creation or his creatures. God is still busy—particularly busy in baptism to finish and perfect what was begun in our birth. We are therefore "born anew" into God's original image for us, redone, recreated, made over, converted, brought forth a second time, "like newborn babes" (1 Pet. 2:2).

New Testament writers knew no way to speak of such radical work in us—unless it is "death"—except to call it "birth."

II

Throughout *How to Be Born Again,* there is no mention of baptism as the model, the norm, the biblical and historic standard by which all our religious experiences are to be judged. Because of this, when the "born-again" experience is talked about by today's Evangelicals, it is often cut off from the church, from the sacraments, or other corporate means of grace. In fact, the emotional, individualized "born-again" experience becomes the new sacrament, the new means of grace. All prior experiences to this inner, heart-felt, once-in-a-lifetime experience, as well as all later growth and outer change, appear to be as nothing without instantaneous personal, cognitive, emotional, inner, penitential acceptance of God's offer of salvation.

But, we ask, can someone be "saved" by baptism alone? Can one be reborn simply by having water splashed over him or her and a few words repeated? Can we equate "rebirth" with "baptism"? Wouldn't that smack of magic, sacerdotalism, and all sorts of other dangerous practices?

This much can be said: It is clear, from the biblical evidence as well as the mainstream of Christian tradition, that the outward rite of baptism and the inward experience of rebirth and renewal are related to one another. But the precise nature of that relationship is open to question. The church has always affirmed that, while the two are related, we cannot say that we cannot be reborn without being baptized. Even the Roman Catholic Church, which firmly says that baptism is necessary for salvation, has traditionally spoken of a "baptism of desire," in which, under certain exceptional circumstances, regeneration takes place without baptism.

If we said that baptism and rebirth are one and the same, we would be simplistically, almost magically, linking the act of baptism with the experience of regeneration. The two are integrally linked. But they are not one and the same. However, on the other hand, neither must we say that baptism is a "mere symbol," "only a ritual" in which something of significance may or may not be present. To speak of baptism in this way is to be clearly at odds with both the biblical testimony on baptism and the church's teaching. Regeneration and baptism are integrally related, but they may not be chronologically related. That is, the rite of baptism and the experience of regeneration may not occur at precisely the same time. One may precede the other in an individual. They may occur at the same moment. Or they may be joined by a lifetime span of years. Remember, we are dealing here, in baptism and in regeneration, with *God's* work; and God works in us in God's own good time and in God's own good way—"The wind blows where it wills."

By far the best way to speak of the "born-again" experience is as a *baptismal* experience. Regeneration is not some inner, exotic, detached phenomenon. Being "born again" is not something which is added to, or happens alongside of, or is optional equipment for baptism. Regeneration is part of baptism. It is one of the gifts, part of the entire phenomenon, another facet of God's work in baptism. And, as has been said from the beginning of this book, baptism is not a momentary rite. *Baptism is a lifetime process of God's work in us.* So is our rebirth in baptism.

III

Few aspects of baptismal spirituality are more foreign to the American evangelical experience of the past century than baptism's stress on conversion, rebirth, regeneration, and salvation as a *process* rather than as a momentary event in a person's life. The religion of the American revivals stresses conversion as a crisis, a moment of awakening, a flash of blinding light which transforms the heart and mind:

> Amazing grace! how sweet the sound
> That saved a wretch like me!
> I once was lost, but now am found,
> Was blind, but now I see.[3]

This moment of rebirth is the initial moment of faith which is celebrated, recalled, and, when the experience fades, is recaptured, and revived again and again throughout the born-again person's life. But all too often, life after that initial moment is neglected. The rest of the old familiar hymn is often forgotten:

> Through many dangers, toils, and snares,
> I have already come;
> 'Tis grace hath brought me safe thus far,
> *And grace will lead me home.* (italics added)

In classical theological terms, justification is emphasized at the expense of sanctification. Most evangelical preaching tirelessly reiterates the first steps of faith with little attention to the rest of the journey.

The idea that rebirth is a momentary, psychologically experienced, once-and-for-all crisis event is foreign both to traditional Protestant theology and to the way baptism depicts conversion. The Protestant Reformers were convinced that sin was so complex, so intricately embedded in human thinking and acting, that only a thousand conversions, a lifetime of turning from sin to God, would root it out. Such sin is not eradicated in four easy steps any more than it is washed in one bath of baptism. It takes a lifetime of repentance and conversion to deal with such sin.

That is why we said in chapter six that salvation, conversion, is best seen as a communal experience, a churchly gift. When the Roman Church used to say, "No salvation outside the church," they were simply trying to affirm our dependence upon the baptizers to help us, throughout our lives, to respond to the promises which we make or which are made for us in baptism. The church is that community of faith which helps us live out the daily, eternal significance of our baptism and daily to appropriate its benefits so that we might eternally live in its light. Our regeneration, our rebirth, our "born againness" is one of those gifts which we receive in the long process of our conversion. But you know how we are—"self-made men and women"—who like to think of our salvation as something we do, rather than something God gives through God's church.

I think of this analogy from my own life. Not long ago I commented, in my mother's presence, that one of the most useful courses I took in high school was typing. I have always been grateful that I knew how to type, and I have used my typing skills every day of my life.

"Aren't you glad that I made you take typing?" my mother said, in an offhand way.

"*Made* me take typing?" I asked in disbelief.

"Yes, I remember it well," she replied. "You didn't think you needed it and thought it would be a waste of time. But I told you it could be helpful in later life. You hated it at first, but I insisted that you stick with it."

I was surprised, to say the least. I was in the process of congratulating myself on my wisdom, my insight, and my forethought in deciding to take a typing course in high school, only to be told that it was not my idea at all. In fact, I had very little to congratulate myself for. My typing skill had come as a gift, the result of someone else's care and direction of me.

The gift of regeneration comes, like all gifts, through people who love us and care for us and guide us toward the Kingdom. Being "born again" is a baptismal experience, part of the process of turning from sin and turning to God. And, for a lifetime, we turn. The promise of baptism is that we are, and will be, born again and again and again and again. That experience of new birth can come later, long after the baptismal rite itself. When it comes, it should be seen as a completion, a perfection, a final carrying out of the promises which were made to us by God at our baptism. Sometimes that rebirth may come before the rite of baptism, sometimes during, sometimes after. But whenever it comes, it comes as part and parcel of the baptismal process, as a gift.

Baptism has long been called the "door" to the faith and the church. That is why many churches traditionally placed their baptismal fonts at the front door of the church—in order to note how one enters through baptism. But sometimes it is difficult to say, at any given moment in our lives, on which side of that "door" we stand. Sometimes we are just taking the handle to open the door, sometimes we are standing upon the threshold, sometimes we are squarely inside with the door behind us. The important thing is that we are on our way in. Baptism says that, wherever you personally stand in relation to this "door" to the faith, it has opened and is being opened for you and you are free to come in.

This is how the church could make the somewhat surprising (surprising to those who think of rebirth as a once-and-for-all experience) statement that even infants are regenerated in their baptism. How can this be? If conversion is defined as a momentary, cognitive, emotional experience, then infants will probably be excluded from that experience. But if conversion is seen as a lifetime of momentous turnings to God, then infants can be participants in that baptismal process. Luther spoke of "infantile faith," an inchoate yet real faith—already present in infants, by God's gift, at baptism. John Calvin said that, while an infant has not fully participated, at his or her baptism, in full repentance and faith, "the seed of both lies hid in them by the secret operation of the spirit" (*Institutes,* Book IV, XVI, 20). After baptizing a baby in the Anglican church, the priest has traditionally addressed the congregation with the words, "Seeing now, dearly beloved brethren, that this child is regenerate. . . ."

Baptismal regeneration of infants only makes sense if baptism is seen not as completed in a moment, but as completed throughout life. In a recent debate on abortion, someone referred to the human fetus as "merely a potential human being." I thought to myself, it is wrong to use the word *merely,* because all of us are "potential human beings." None of us is finished when he or she emerges from the womb. God's image in us is forever being formed in us. No matter how powerful one's baptism or how soul-shaking one's later conversion experience, only a lifetime of death and rebirth can work so radical a transformation as God intends for his "new creations." So, John Calvin could say that our being "born again" in baptism "does not take place in one moment, or one day or one year; but through continual and, sometimes even slow advances" (*Institutes*, Book III, III, 9).

But we want it all, instantly, in the snap of a finger, in the twinkling of an eye. We want to be converted, made over, redone, saved without effort, without cost or pain. But God's transformation is not wrought in us so quickly or painlessly. It takes time, God's own good time. Today, the gospel is often presented as "the best deal a man ever had," (to quote Oral Roberts) as the answer to all human problems, as the easy remedy for whatever ails us. But the gospel calls for nothing less radical nor anything less painful than birth itself. And most births come with some pain.

IV

But having said all this about the promises and the process of baptism, I do not mean to deny that God's work of rebirth in us demands our yes. Billy Graham is completely correct on that point. While God's work in us is not limited nor initiated by our actions, beliefs, and decisions, God's work in us is of little consequence without our reception of that work, without our yes. God's thundering yes to us in Christ has little practical meaning without our yes to him in our lives. I think American Evangelicals have been wrong in their insistence on one pattern of rebirth for everybody, in their view of conversion as a subjective once-and-for-all event, and in their one-sided emphasis upon human feelings, human beliefs, human decisions for salvation with too little emphasis upon God's work in our salvation. But the evangelicals could not be more right in their insistence that God's gift demands our response. A gift which is offered and not received may still be a gift—but, because it is not received, it is also a tragedy.

While our rebirth may be sudden or slow, wildly emotional or quiet and reserved, while it may be something we can document as to the place and hour and day, or may be something which came upon us quietly, in the process of many days and hours; nevertheless we must be reborn. It is not so much a question of whether we can say *when* this rebirth happens to us, as it is a question of whether we can now say that we have begun, by faith, to live the life and death of Jesus Christ in our own lives. For Luther, rebirth was not so much an *experience* as a *fact* which has happened to us in baptism and which now is simply to be believed and lived. As Luther says somewhere to those who were unduly

91

anxious about their salvation, "This new life cannot be experienced but must be believed. For no one knows that he lives again or experiences that he is justified, but he believes and hopes."

Assent is required. There is no Christian without response to Christ. That response is both conscious and intentional. It is not so much a one-time response as a lifetime of responsiveness and responsibility. I agree with John Baillie who noted, in *Baptism and Conversion,* that "decisions" for Christ may be made in different ways by different people and that they are usually made more than once. But however and whenever they are made, they must be made. "We don't fall up the spiritual stairs. We climb them one step at a time. And the steps are acts of conscious commitment of the whole self to the God we meet in Jesus Christ" (p. 112).

Baptism is incomplete, fragmented, inconclusive without the response of the one who is baptized. Daily we turn to the One who turned to us in our baptism. Daily we keep the promises we make in baptism in response to God's promise. Sometimes that response is life-changing and soul-shaking. Sometimes it is quiet and reasoned. Sometimes it is a conscious decision and sometimes it is an unconscious response to the mystery of God's work in our lives. We respond when we decide how to spend money, when we vote, when we come forward for Communion. But at sometime or another, the response must be conscious, felt, known, definite and intentional. At some point we must clearly say yes.

But when we say yes, even our yes is a work of God's grace in us. A gift. We are merely saying yes to who God has created and is creating us to be. The old is passing away, the new is being born in us. We say yes to that strange birth which has been ours from the beginning. David Steinmetz called to my attention that the reformer Huldreich Zwingli compared baptism to the monk's cowl or uniform which is given to a novice when he joins a monastic order. The young boy of twelve is a monk from the moment he accepts the uniform and the obligations which wearing it entails. But he is not, at age twelve, a monk in the same sense as the old brother of eighty-two who has been wearing the uniform for lo these many years. The young boy must grow to the uniform he has been given. Baptism is our uniform into which we must grow. It is cut for a far more generously proportioned person than we are now. But we will grow up into it as we are continuously, daily converted into ever deeper levels of devotion to God. Conversion does not supplant or bypass baptism. It fits us to it. It enables us to grow into baptism's image for us, so that in being born and growing up in Christ we come to possess everything which God offered us in baptism, and we find that we have become all that we profess.

Those of us who have been born and are being born again expectantly await God's work to be completed within us so that on the last day of our lives and our first day of eternity we can look back upon our lives and see—God's promised "new creation" in *us!*

And you come forth from death into eternity, sticky, kicking, squalling, and fresh—like a newborn baby from its mama's womb.

Write a statement defending your rebirth to someone who asks you if you are born again.

93

9. Death by Drowning

Make a list of all the things water signifies to you, that is, everything you associate with water.

Do you not know that all of us who have been baptized into Christ Jesus were baptized into his death?—Rom.6:3-5

I

Whenever anybody asks me, "What does baptism mean?" I always respond, "Baptism means everything which water means." But then, when I ask, "What does water mean?" I receive answers such as, "cleansing," "refreshment," "life." In this book you have seen that all of these images are both true to our experience of water and are also true to New Testament ways of speaking about baptism. But even these rich images do not say enough, for they overlook the primary New Testament way of speaking about baptism. Baptism is *death*.

The early church often built its baptismal fonts in the shape of *tombs*. In this way it reminded itself of something we moderns often forget: Water is not only the source, origin, and sustainer of life, it is also the potential terminator of life. Our bodies contain several gallons of water—but only a teaspoon or so in the wrong place brings instant, suffocating, terrifying death. We are born in the water, with fins and gills—but we are also born with a deep, primordial fear of death by drowning.

Sometimes we moderns romaticize water. We speak of water as natural, fresh, and refreshing. But old Israel knew better. For the children of Abraham, water was a thing to be dreaded: the surging, dark, bubbling chaos of nothingness and death. In Genesis, when God began creating, the first necessary act of creation was to tame the waters. A "firmament" was needed to separate the waters above from the waters below so that dry land might appear (1:6-9). And it was good.

In the other creation story of Genesis 2, a river gives life to Eden, but a few chapters later, that same river of life becomes a surging torrent of death and destruction. Noah goes into the ark and watches as the death waters rise, forever rise, during those dark, wet forty days and forty nights while "God wiped out every living thing that existed on earth" (Gen. 7:23, NEB).

Yet, it was upon those same waters of death that Noah, his family, and the creatures in the ark were preserved until there was once again dry land upon which to stand. Life began again as the death waters receded and a rainbow arched across the sky in testimony to a new covenant: Never again need the earth fear annihilation by water.

But water continued to be a primary biblical image for death and destruction. The psalmist, describing himself "sunk in misery," cries out:

Deep calls to deep in the roar of thy cataracts, and all thy waves, all thy breakers, pass over me (Psalm 42:7, NEB).

Let other nations put their ships to sea and sing of the glories of the ocean. As for Israel, she preferred dry ground, the solid and sure footing of the promised *land*.

II

And so it is with great interest that we watch as Jesus appears on the banks of the Jordan and asks to be plunged into the river by John. John, like the prophets before him, prepares the way. He is a pre-Christian figure who points the way to the one who is to come. The preparation which John urges is a "baptism of repentance." People are to repent and be baptized, to get ready for the coming Messiah. John's baptism is presented as a preparatory, temporary stage in God's dealings with his world: "I have baptized you with water," John warns. "But he will baptize you with fire."

But why was Jesus baptized by John? What did Jesus need to prepare for or repent of? Past Christians worried over questions about the sinfulness of Christ which are raised by his baptism. I will not deal with these past arguments here except to say that Jesus affirms John's baptism on its own terms (Mark

11:30). He affirms John's baptism as relating to sin and repentance.

However, Jesus' baptism is much more than mere washing and repentance. As was stated in chapter five, when Jesus is baptized by John, John's baptism is transformed from a sign of *human* preparedness to an occasion for *divine* activity. The heavens open, the Spirit descends, a claim is made. The baptism of Jesus is a sign that there is now nothing more for which to wait or to prepare—God is present in Christ. The baptism of Jesus is not a ritual of preparation but rather a ritual of inauguration. The kingdom of God is present, in the midst of us, in the presence of the one who is shown, through this baptism, to be God's son in whom he is well pleased.

But in what *way* is Jesus the near presence of God? His baptism is the revelation not only of Jesus' identity as the awaited Messiah but also of the unexpected way he will be the Messiah. This Messiah comes not (as some were expecting) as a military overlord. He comes as a servant. He is the obedient servant, "fulfilling all righteousness," more than he is the ruling master. In his baptism is revealed the pattern of his entire ministry. In being baptized by John, Jesus identifies himself in solidarity with sinners. He shows forth the surprising lordship of the Lord who is servant to those whom he has come to save.

And what is the nature of that service which this savior comes to render? Jesus' baptism is also the revelation of that. On two different occasions, Jesus himself uses the word *baptism* to refer to his own impending *death*. He asks his wayward disciples, "Can you drink the cup that I drink, or be baptized with the baptism I am baptized with"? (Mark 10:38, NEB) And, as he moves steadily toward the cross, Jesus says, "I have a baptism to be baptized with; and how I am constrained until it is accomplished!" (Luke 12:50) Jesus forges the link between his baptism and his death. His death on the cross is his submission, his obedience even unto death, his "baptism." Jesus thus symbolizes, as he submits to John's baptism in the Jordan, the radical way in which he will confront the sin which enslaves humanity, meeting it on its own turf, submitting even to death in order to save through his servanthood—a servanthood even unto death.

In other words, John's baptism, while not erased by Christ, is given much deeper meaning as Christ himself submits to baptism.

96

In Christ, the repentance, the "turning around," which John called for is intensified, even to the point of death. John may have presented his baptism as the washing away of sins, but Jesus seeks a more radical confrontation with sin than a cleansing bath. He seeks nothing less than *death*. In the baptism of his church, a new chapter in the story of God's dealings with his people is initiated. In this New Age, a servant is sent who is God himself, in the flesh, who will go down and defeat evil in its own territory, as a life-and-death encounter.

This may account for why we have no record that Jesus or his disciples baptized anyone during his earthly ministry. Jesus' proclamation was not a simple call to preparatory repentance in the sense that John preached repentance. Rather, Jesus' own baptism was the beginning of an obedient ministry which would not be fulfilled until he was obedient even unto the cross. Baptism was the beginning of his death, the first visible indication of the radical quality of his servanthood. Jesus and his disciples did not baptize because it was not yet time. Before the completion of his earthly ministry and crucifixion, Jesus had not yet made everything ready for his Kingdom. The full dealings of God with the world had not yet been accomplished, the process of Jesus' own "baptism" had not been fulfilled, so his disciples were not yet ready to begin baptizing.

It was at the cross and the tomb that Jesus' "baptism" was finally accomplished. There his saving work, begun and foreshadowed at his own baptism in the Jordan, was finally done. The last enemy was met and defeated. God's love for the world was fully revealed. His teaching and preaching were made visible. The depth and seriousness of human sin, the subtlety and power of evil as well as the depth and power of God's love, met and were fully revealed upon the cross. "It is accomplished," Jesus victoriously and obediently pronounced from the cross as he died.

Now, Jesus' saving work having been done, his own "baptismal" process having been completed, Jesus commands his disciples to begin *their* saving work:

Go therefore and make disciples of all nations, baptizing them in the name of the Father and of the Son and of the Holy Spirit.

(Matt. 28:19)

97

The disciples are now to go and "make disciples." How are disciples made? Disciples are made by "baptism" and "teaching" (Matt. 28:20). In Acts, after the "pouring out of the Spirit" and the birthday of the church (Acts 2), at the end of Peter's Pentecost sermon to the wondering crowd, when the crowd asks, "What must we do to be saved?" Peter's response is simple:

> Repent, and be baptized every one of you in the name of Jesus Christ for the forgiveness of your sins; and you shall receive the gift of the Holy Spirit (Acts 2:38-39).

Baptism is the passageway into discipleship, the fitting response to the proclamation of the gospel, the model for what the Christian life is: a life of obedience, servanthood, love, and faithfulness—even unto death.

But even if Christ were baptized, even if his baptism signified his servanthood unto death and his obedient solidarity with sinful humanity unto death, why would his disciples understand themselves as commanded to continue the practice of baptism? In what way is baptism seen as initiation into the kingdom of God and as passageway to discipleship?

There is no better place to see the early church's understanding of baptism than in the writings of Paul. For Paul, as we have seen in earlier chapters, baptism is many things—adoption, birth, cleansing, circumcision, and light. But above all, baptism is *death*. In coming forth for baptism, in "submitting" as Jesus submitted to John, the believer, Paul says, shows that he or she is truly "in Christ," that is, that he or she is *in the same death-rising process as Christ*. Paul reminds those Colossians who continue to dabble in "elemental spirits" and human "philosophies" that such pre-baptismal paganism will not do. "You were circumcised," he tells them. Like the children of the old Israel, you were initiated into a new status, a new way of living. What is this "circumcision of Christ"? It is baptism.

> *You were buried with him in baptism,* in which you were also raised with him through faith in the working of God, who raised him from the dead. And you, who were dead . . . God made alive together with him, . . . He disarmed the principalities and powers and made a public example of them, triumphing over them in him (Col. 2:12-15, italics added).

98

Baptism brings death, death to our old ways of thinking and acting. As Paul told the Colossians, "For you have died, and your life is hid with Christ in God" (Col. 3:3).

In chapter five of his letter to the Romans, Paul eloquently testifies to the free, unmerited grace of God in Christ. But in chapter six, he qualifies his statement on grace by speaking to those who misinterpret what this free grace means by asking, "If grace is so free, why not sin all the more so that God can spread around more grace?" (Col. 6:1).

For Paul, the person who asks such a question has forgotten the meaning of baptism:

> How can we who died to sin still live in it? Do you not know that *all of us who have been baptized into Christ Jesus were baptized into his death? We were buried therefore with him by baptism into death,* so that as Christ was raised from the dead by the glory of the Father, we too might walk in newness of life.
> For if we have been united with him in a death like his, we shall certainly be united with him in a resurrection like his. . . . *Our old self was crucified with him so that the sinful body might be destroyed, and we might no longer be enslaved to sin. For he who has died is freed from sin. . . . So you also must consider yourselves dead to sin and alive to God in Christ Jesus* (Rom. 6:2-11, italics added).

The fruits of baptism are essentially a changed life "in Christ." The one who is baptized is a "new creation" in which the old sinful body and its old servitude no longer hold the person. We are dead to that old self and "alive to Christ."

There is a marked difference between saying "be clean" and saying "be dead and reborn." Christian baptism is not merely a repeatable washing of someone so that he or she can be clean enough to achieve personal immortality. Baptism is nothing less than *death* and nothing more than the creation of a new being who lives by a radically different system of obedience, servanthood, and community. Behind every baptism is the "baptism" of Jesus, his death and resurrection, which opened up the New Age. Paul simply drew out clearly the relationship between Jesus' baptism and death and our baptism "into Christ"—as well as the ethical implications of this relationship.

Whenever Paul speaks about the work of Christ in us, he seems

not to know whether to speak in terms of "birth" or "death"—
baptism "into Christ" felt like being killed and being born at the
same time.

III

The early Fathers continued to be impressed by the death-life
dynamic of the baptismal experience. In fourth-century
Jerusalem, Cyril, in his postbaptismal instruction, explained to
the newly baptized:

> Then you were led to the holy pool of Divine Baptism, as Christ
> taken down from the cross was laid in the tomb already prepared.
> Each one was questioned. . . . You made the profession of salvation
> and three times were you plunged in the water and came forth,
> signifying Christ's burial for three days. By this action, you died and
> you were born, and for you the saving water was at once a grave and
> the womb of a mother (*Lectures on the Christian Sacraments,*
> XXXIII, 1080, C, English trans.).

In the Western church, Ambrose also explained baptism as death:

> Whoever is baptized, is baptized in the death of Christ. What does
> this mean: "in the death"? That, as Christ died, you also must taste
> death: as Christ died to sin and lives for God, so you also must die to
> the past pleasures of sin by the sacrament of baptism, and rise again
> by the grace of Christ. . . . When you plunge into the water, you
> receive the likeness of death and burial. You receive the sacrament
> of His cross. . . . And you, when you are crucified, you are joined
> to Christ, you are joined to the gift of Our Lord Jesus Christ (*Des
> Sacraments,* II, 23, my translation).

Baptism was usually done during the night before Easter, at
least until the early Middle Ages. Baptism during the Christian
Passover not only provided a linkage of our "death" in baptism
with Christ's passion and death, but also beautifully symbolized
our "passover" from slavery to freedom, from death to life, from
darkness to light in baptism.

The reformers were also impressed with the death-life theme of
baptism. In his *Small Catechism,* Luther asks, "What does baptism mean for daily living?"

It means that our old sinful self, with all its evil deeds and desires, should be drowned through daily repentance; and that day after day a new self should arise to live with God in righteousness and purity forever (p. 42).

In baptism the "old Adam" is drowned. But, as Luther observed elsewhere, "The old Adam is a mighty good swimmer." As we said in the last chapter, the Protestant Reformers were convinced that our sin is so complex and deep rooted that only a thousand conversions and a lifetime of repentings would root it out— nothing less than death will do.

Repentance and *conversion* are best understood as baptismal words. When we repent, we merely ask God who has buried us in baptism to continue the work of putting us to death. We volunteer for death. We turn to God, each day, like little children, and say, "I can't save myself. You must do it for me." "I can't be good. Make me good." "I can't preserve my life. Take my life and hide it in your love." This is repentance talk which is also baptismal-death talk. The reformers speak of repentance as a daily return to baptism. Everyday of our lives we have to wake up in order to die—to continue the work begun in us at baptism. We never get too old or too pure or too righteous to be exempt from the need to die to our old selves and rise to Christ.

Our conversion is therefore a continuing, day-to-day living out of the death-life experience which begins at our baptism, asking God to do for us what we can never do for ourselves, to finish the saving work in us which was begun at baptism. Baptism is a once-and-for-all sacrament which takes one's whole life to finish. As we said in the last chapter, it is a process more than a moment. Conversion is part of the baptismal process with a final goal no less than the total refashioning of our sinful, disobedient, proud selves into more what God intended for us. It is birth which comes through death. You do not get so radical a transformation in a moment. It takes a lifetime of death and resurrection to make so radical a change.

As the old baptismal prayers in the *Book of Common Prayer,* 1559, said it:

O Merciful God, grant that the old Adam in these children may be so buried, that the new man may be raised up in them. Amen.

101

Grant that all carnal affections may die in them, and that all things belonging to the Spirit may live and grow in them. Amen.

Grant that they may have power and strength to have victory, and to triumph against the devil, the world, and the flesh. Amen. (p. 274)

How different is the understanding of the Christian life in these prayers from that which is held in some Christian circles today where the gospel is offered as the solution for human problems, the fulfillment of human expectations, and a good way to make nice people even nicer. These baptismal prayers speak of Christian life as the beginning of problems, the destruction of our expectations for human self-fulfillment, the ultimate challenge to our delusions of goodness.

Baptism says that our problem is not that we have a few minor moral adjustments which need to be made in us so that we can be good. Our problem is that we are so utterly enslaved that nothing less than a full-scale, lifelong conversion will do. Nothing less than daily, sometimes painful, often frightening death will do. As my colleague at Duke, David Steinmetz, wrote in the April, 1978, issue of *Theology Today:*

> Every conversion has a price. Something is gained, but something is lost as well and the loss may prove to be painful . . . The gospel not only resolves problems which trouble us; it creates problems which we never had before and which we would gladly avoid ("Reformation and Conversion," p. 31).

There is a wrath and judgment of God which is poured upon us along with God's acceptance and love. He may take me "just as I am without one plea," but he will not let me be until he has finished what he has begun in my baptism. Sometimes God's work in me is painful. But God destroys our old decadent selves, buries our past, sweeps through our prejudices, inundates our self-centeredness not simply to destroy. Death comes in order that a new reality, a new being may take its place. The death is for the sake of life, and that dying and rising is a daily affair.

IV

The newest doors of Saint Peter's in Rome are the great bronze doors of the sculptor, Giacomo Manzu, the artist friend of John

XXIII. On one door is depicted a series of death scenes, "Death by Falling," "Death in War," and others. "Death by Water" is also there. To some it may seem strange to welcome people into this great church with images of death upon the front door. But we must. We must speak of death first, in the same way as the church often placed its baptismal fonts at the front door. This reminds us that to be baptized, to enter the church, is to volunteer for *death*—again and again and again.

The striking Argentinian Evangelical Juan Carlos Ortiz often uses this baptismal formula when he baptizes: "*I kill* you in the name of the Father, and of the Son, and of the Holy Spirit, and *I make you born* into the kingdom of God to serve him and to please him." It is rather shocking, but so is baptism!

Sometimes I wonder, in most of our celebrations of baptism, if we reduce the waters of baptism to a mere sprinkle, and cover it up with rosebuds and lace and talk about cute babies and "God loves you and we love you" because we dare not speak about that strange and wonderful work which is beginning in this child on this day. You know how we always try to avoid *death*.

Baptism is death which leads to life. "For you have died," Paul says, in the past tense, "and your life is hid with Christ in God," speaking in the present and future tense. We live as dead people who have lost all hope in the world so that we might live as those who know they have been raised in order to be claimed as God's own.

To be baptized is to be condemned to die. It is dress rehearsal for the last day of your life as well as for every day in which we must die to all that would make us less than God wants for us. Baptism is also resurrection practice. Between our death in baptism and our next death at the end of our earthly life, we live in the hope that the same God who raised us from the waters of baptism will raise us again, pulling us forth from the tomb like newborn babes come from the womb. We live in confidence which comes from baptism, because we have already been through a trial run of our death and resurrection. We do not fear death, because we need not fear what we have already done.

We should be giving mouth-to-mouth resuscitation to a child at baptism rather than kissing it on the cheek. Death is starting to happen.

103

Pity the poor baby at baptism, he may not know it, but he has only begun to die!

But in that death is life.

Draw in each segment of this crest a representation of something we need to die to in our baptism.

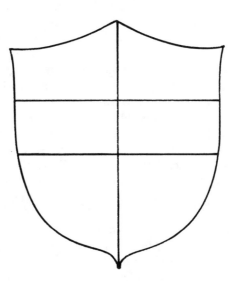

10. Remember Who You Are

Write your name in full and explain the history
of your name and how you received it.

*The Lord called me from the womb, from the body of my
mother he named my name.—Isa. 49:1*

I

Back in high school, every Friday and Saturday night,
as I was leaving home to go on a date, I remember my mother
bidding me farewell at the front door with these weighty words,
"Don't forget who you are."

You know what she meant. She did not mean that I was in
danger of forgetting my name and my street address. She meant
that, alone on a date, in the midst of some party, in the presence of
some strangers, I might forget who I was. I might lose sight of the
values with which I had been raised, answer to some alien name,
engage in some unaccustomed behavior.

"Don't forget who you are," was her maternal benediction as I
left home.

It is sometimes difficult in modern life, amidst the conflicting
claims and confusion of names, to remember who we are. We are
forever answering to some false name, forever misunderstanding
who we are and by whom we are named. It is easy to forget.

I have sympathy with youth today. "Who am I?" is a particularly pressing question for youth. The search for the self, the quest
for one's identity consumes much of our teenage years. And today
there are a myriad of causes, groups, philosophies, and cults
which are willing and ready to tell us who we are.

Who am I?

"You are mostly a sexual being," the movies, soap operas, and
songs tell you. "You are lusting and being lusted after. Your body

105

Font at St. John the Baptist
New Brighton, Minnesota

is your most important possession; nurture it, love it, display it, caress it, show it off. You are heterosexual, homosexual, craving, satisfaction seeking, orgasm needing, sexual object and pursuer, getting ready for a lifetime of affairs, trysts, rendezvous, and romance.''

Who am I?

''You are mostly a brain, mostly a rational, thinking, reasoning being; absorbing facts and figures, going to school—endless school—bowing down before the temples of Athena, living only to learn, not learning to live. Knowledge is power, so you had better get as much as possible. It's not who you are but what you know,'' the schools tell our children through twelve plus years of education.

Who am I?

''You are mostly maker and spender of money, capitalist, doer, producer, coveter, obtainer of stereo, car with bucket seats and racing stripes, preparing for your first mortgage in suburbia with a two-car garage and forty-year payments,'' the advertizers and peddlers tell us.

Who am I?

''You are the self-centered, autonomous, self-made being,'' this modern, scientific, secular world tells us. ''Nobody will look out for you but you. You are the most important project in your life; nurture, care for, and love your adorable 'me.' There are no values save the ones you create. No meaning save the meaning you choose. Look out for number one, satisfy, soothe, make happy, thrill, care for your lonely little 'me.' ''

And the answers go on and on. We all know them, and many of us have bought into them. The truth is that the identity question of ''Who am I?'' is no longer over and done with by age twenty-one. I know people in their thirties, their fifties, who still ask the question, still experiment with their lives, mixing in this and that, hoping the whole thing will jell before it blows up in their faces. They do not answer always to the same name, because the names keep changing. Like Proteus, the hero of Greek mythology who could change his shape at will, we continually change our shapes to suit the situation, going through endless Protean metamorphoses as the situation demands. In *Passages,* Gail Sheehy tells it all, this continuing, never-ending, lifelong crisis of identity; the

"Who am I?" asked all the way from womb to tomb, through one passage to the next.

II

To the pressing "Who am I?" question, the church has traditionally responded, *"You are baptized."*

In this book I have spoken of baptism as the norm, the model, the pattern, the beginning and end of the Christian life. In baptism, God acts through the church, in water, to enlarge the family of God and to save them by joining them to the death and resurrection of Christ. In baptism we are initiated, crowned, chosen, embraced, washed, adopted, gifted, reborn, killed, and thereby sent forth and redeemed. We are identified as one of God's own, then assigned our place and our job within the kingdom of God.

The way for a Christian to find out who he or she is, is not to jump on the rear of a Honda and head west, but rather to come to the font and look into those graceful waters. The reflection of yourself which you see there is who you really are.

Who am I?

"You are someone to whom *a name is given.*"

"What name shall be given to this child?" the minister has traditionally asked when a child is brought to the font. This act of "christening" was the bestowal of the Christian name (as opposed to the child's family name) upon the child by the church. In ancient times, the church literally named the child, often in memory of some favorite saint. The naming is reminiscent of the time when a person's name was changed after a conversion experience or some dramatic change in a person's life. In the Bible, Abram's name was changed to Abraham when he received God's promise to make of him a great nation. Cephas became Peter, when Christ promised to build his church "upon this rock." Saul, knocked down on the Damascus Road, became Paul the apostle. The names change to symbolize a new beginning, a radical break with the old.

Generally, our names are given to us. Many people, in spite of their "official" names, are given nicknames by their friends. A person can choose his or her own name and, through a legal process, make that name his or her own. But this is not the normal way names come to us. Normally, a name is a gift.

Life becomes a long process of trying that name on for size, growing up to it, answering to it, giving it meaning by the way we live our lives. At first, a big name like William, Catherine, Elizabeth, or Arthur will sound strange when set upon a wee infant. But the child will grow to the name, filling it out, until one day it feels natural, it fits, and we could not imagine the person with any other name.

Whether one's name is actually given in the rite of baptism or not (which is usually not the case today), baptism continues to be an occasion for naming. At baptism we are given the name, "Christian." That name, at whatever age it is given, is a gift—unearned, unmerited, undeserved—like salvation itself.

In so doing, the church makes a radically different statement about who we are and how we get to be who we are. We are telling the baptized person that his or her identity is *a gift,* a corporate endowment of the church, something bestowed upon you by grace. We—who have been taught of late that identity is a personal discovery, the end result of rooting about in the dark recesses of our own egos, or our fleeting glimpses of ourselves as we drift from one momentary high to another—will be shocked to learn that identity is given rather than earned.

We did not "discover" our identity as a member of a human family nor did we earn our family name. We got them as gifts. We learned who we were through the day-to-day love and care which our families showed us. We learn what it is to be called by the name "Christian" in the same way. A baby at six months may not bear the name "Christian" in the same way as the old saint of sixty years. But give the new Christian time and he or she will grow to his or her name and it will fit him or her fine.

How idiotic (and uncaring) of modern society to tell its young, in effect, "We have no values, nothing to pass on to you, no claim upon your life, no name. You go out and find your own identity." No wonder so many get lost along the way.

How insensitive and unfaithful of today's church to tell its young, in effect, "We have no values, nothing to pass on to you, no story, no claim upon your life, no name, no mission." In so doing we produce adolescents of twenty and thirty years, paralyzed by anxiety, cast adrift upon a sea of moral relatives, answering to any ideology or cult which promises them an identity strong enough to overwhelm their own lack of purpose and direction. The church anxiously awaits the growing child's decision as to whether he or she will accept the church as mother or not, timidly wondering what it can do to "attract the youth" or "turn them on." So the church builds a new gymnasium or takes its young on a trip to Disney World and dares to call it "youth ministry." The youth, who often either yawn or go elsewhere, at least have the good sense to know not to ask identity from those who know not themselves who they are.

I pray for the time when the church again courageously embraces her young at the font and proclaims, "This one is *ours*. This one belongs to *us*. God has big plans for this one. This one is set aside for *God*. We're calling this one 'Christian.'"

Who am I?

Baptism says not only that we are the ones to whom a name has been given but also we are *royalty*.

We sin, of course. And we live less righteously than we should. But our sin, our unrighteousness is significant and troubling only because we know that we were made for something better. Our sin is noteworthy, our inhumanity is blasphemous, only because it does not befit the character of ones so worthy! Worthy, because we have been made worthy—bought, adopted, made heir, elevated by the King of kings himself.

The Christian message is not that we should try hard to "act like somebody." The Christian message is simply, "We *are* somebody." The church does not rest as long as even one of God's heirs is in misery, hungry, naked, oppressed, persecuted, lost. We do not rest as long as any institution, government, or person seeks to warp or distort God's royal image in any of God's children.

The trouble with much of our social activism is that it often starts with, "What can the church do to serve the world?" So the church ends up running errands for whatever the world happens to be craving at the moment. Not all action in the world is *God's* action. We should begin as the baptized and the baptizers asking, "How can the church serve the imperative of the gospel (to "go into all the world . . . baptizing") and thereby help the world discover its true identity as *God's* world, God's cherished creation?" On the other hand, the trouble with much of our evangelism is that it often starts with, "What can the church do to save individuals?" So the church ends up speaking to individuals, pleading for inner change, ignoring outward needs and pressures, corporate evil, social injustice. Salvation is thus reduced to the personal, the therapeutic, the subjective, the emotional, the individual and is thus made petty and local. Our baptismal mandate is more cosmic, more "worldly" than that. Our evangelism and social activism are one in speaking and doing the Good News to God's cherished heirs. This is all baptismal work, and we had best be about that work with vigor.

Who am I?

Baptism says not only that we are named and that we are royalty but also that *we are owned by God forever.*

In earlier chapters we spoke of baptism as if it were a branding, a sealing of someone as God's property. God keeps what God purchases, and on the cross an awesome price was paid.

In times of great doubt, when struggling through his dark nights of the soul, Martin Luther would sometimes touch his forehead and say to himself, "Martin, be calm, you are baptized." In times of our doubt, inner turmoil, hopelessness, and confusion we, too, would do well to touch our foreheads, where the sign and seal of baptism was made, and remember our baptism. One of the appealing features of the new baptismal rites is the provision for periodic services of baptismal renewal. These new services provide opportunities for individuals, or entire congregations, to remember their baptism. [4]

Once God, through the church, has claimed us in baptism, God does not let us go easily. A few summers ago, a boy in our church returned home from his first year at college. He appeared at my office to tell me that I would not be seeing him at church while he was home over the summer. When I asked why, he told me, "Well, you see I have been doing a lot of thinking about religion while I was at college, and I have come to the conclusion that there is not much to this religion thing. I have found out that I don't need the church to get by," he said.

I responded by saying I found all that interesting.

"Aren't you worried? I thought you would go through the roof when I told you," he said.

I had known this boy for about five years, had baptized him a couple of years ago on profession of faith, and had watched him grow during his high school years. He came from a difficult family situation. The church had been very interested in him and had a hand in making it possible for him to go to college.

"No, I'm interested, but not overly concerned. I'll be watching to see if you can pull it off," I told him.

"What do you mean 'pull it off'? I don't understand. I'm nineteen. I can decide to do anything I want to do, can't I?"

"When I was nineteen I thought I was 'on my own,' too. I'm saying that I'm not so sure you will be able to get away with this," I said—to the increasingly confused young man.

"Why not?" he asked.

"Well, for one thing, you're baptized."

"So what does that have to do with anything?"

"Well, you try forsaking it, rejecting it, forgetting about it, and maybe you'll find out," I suggested.

"I can't figure out what being baptized has to do with me," he said.

"For one thing, there are people here who care about you. They made promises to God when you were baptized. You try not showing up around here this summer, and they will be nosing around, asking you what you are doing with your life, what kind of grades you made last semester, what you're doing with yourself. Then there's also God. No telling what God might try with you. From what I've seen of God, once he has claimed you, you don't get off the hook so easily. God is relentless in claiming what is his. And, in baptism, God says you belong to him."

The boy shook his head in wonder at this strange, unreasonable brand of ecclesiastical reasoning and more or less stumbled out the door of my study. In a week or so, he was back at his usual place on the second pew. The baptizers had done their work. God's possessiveness had remained firm. Somewhere C. S. Lewis says that he feels sorry for atheists. He feels sorry for people who try to live their lives without God, because, in Lewis's words, "God is so resourceful, so unscrupulous in keeping his own." In baptism, God tells me that he owns *me* and that he will keep me.

Remembering our baptism, we remember who we are and *whose* we are.

III

In Alex Haley's book, *Roots,* there is a memorable scene the night the slave, Kunta Kinte, drove his master to a ball at a big plantation house. Kunta Kinte heard the music from inside the house, music from the white folk's dance. He parked the buggy and settled down to wait out the long night of his master's revelry. While he sat in the buggy, he heard other music coming from the slaves' quarters, the little cabins behind the big house. It was different music, music with a different rhythm. He felt his legs carrying him down the path toward those cabins. There he found a man playing African music, *his* music which he remembered hearing in Africa as a child—the music he had almost forgotten. Kunta Kinte found that the man was from his section of Africa. They talked excitedly, in his native language, of home and the things of home.

That night, after returning from the dance, Kunta Kinte went home changed. He lay upon the dirt floor of his little cabin and wept, weeping in sadness that he had almost forgotten, weeping in joy that he had at last remembered. The terrifying, degrading experience of slavery had almost obliterated his memory of who he was. But the music had helped him remember.

Jesus said there was once a boy who left home, saying to his father, "Give me what I deserve and I will leave this place." The boy went out from his father's house and into a "far country" where he wasted himself and his inheritance in loose living. He began living like a pig. And then, one day, Jesus said, the boy came to his senses. The boy said, "Wait a minute. What am I doing out here in this far country living like a pig, starving to death, groveling like a slave? I have a father. I've got a home."

The boy remembered who he was. He remembered home. That remembering, that "coming to himself" as Jesus described it, put his feet back on the path toward home. At the moment he remembered, he did not become his father's son for the first time. He did not suddenly become something he was not. Rather, he remembered who he was. As Cardinal Newman said of his conversion, "I knew, but until then I did not know that I knew."

I take this parable to be a baptismal parable. It is a parable of how easy it is, in the midst of this life, to forget who you are and whose you are. So the church is here to remind you, to remind one another, that we have been bought with a price, that someone greater than us has named us and claimed us and seeks us and loves us with only one good reason in mind—so that he might love us for all eternity.

Remember *your* baptism and be thankful, for this is who you are.

Write a prayer of thanksgiving for the person you are, the person God has made you.

Notes

1. *La tradition apostolique de saint Hippolyte essai de reconstruction,* trans. Dom Bernard Botte (Munster Westfalen: Aschendorff Verlagsbuch—handlung, 1963). The following passage is my English translation of a section from the above.

2. I am indebted to Robert W. Jenson's article, "The Mandate and Promise of Baptism," *Interpretation* (July, 1976, vol. XXX, No. 3), pp. 271-287 for helping me to organize the following thoughts on baptism and the Holy Spirit.

3. John Newton, "Amazing Grace," 1831.

4. A service of *Baptism, Confirmation, and Renewal* (Nashville: Abingdon, 1976).

An Educational Guide
for a Church School Class
or Adult Study Group

The chapters in this book are presented for easy use in a ten-week course for adults. What follows is an educational guide for the use of groups. If you prefer, you could also use the individual exercises at the beginning and end of each chapter as preparation and class activities for a group. The following educational guide, which is arranged to be used in a ten-week course, can also be adapted for a six-week Lenten study group. If you choose the latter option, you will need to combine Chapters 2 and 3, 4 and 5, 6 and 7, and 8 and 9; Chapters 1 and 10 can be used as presented. Before you proceed, read the following guide and either choose particular preparation exercises and class sessions or combine them.

Preparation

Before your first class meeting have one or two of your group interview your pastor. Ask the following questions:

When do we celebrate baptisms?
What requirements do we have?
How do we prepare persons for baptism?
What does baptism mean to you?

Also secure copies of your church's most recent baptismal liturgy for each member of your class. Read Chapter 1 before class.

1. The Rock from Whence You Were Hewn

When you meet, report on your interview. Pass out and read aloud your church's most recent baptismal liturgy. Compare and contrast these with the description of baptism discussed in this chapter. Make a list on newsprint of the questions you now have about the nature and meaning of baptism. Place these on the wall for use during the sessions which follow.

In preparation for your next session have each person observe and describe the experiences children have in your church and home. Reflect on your description and then state what self-understanding a child is likely to learn from these experiences. Read Chapter 2.

2. Royalty

Begin by sharing your observations and implied learnings. Discuss the similarities and differences between your findings and those defended in this chapter. Then attempt to formulate in your own words your group's convictions on who we are as baptized Christians. Finally, make a list of implications for family and church life.

In preparation for the next session have groups of three to six persons choose a biblical text and write a short two-to-three page baptismal sermon. Read Chapter 3.

3. The Chosen

Share the sermons each group has written. Discuss them in the light of Chapter 3. Together write an insert for your church bulletin explaining baptism.

In preparation for the next session ask each person to prepare a guide to Christian child rearing. Read Chapter 4.

4. Come On In, the Water's Fine

Share your guides to Christian child rearing. Discuss them in the light of Chapter 3. Together prepare a guide to be handed out to parents in your congregation who wish to have their children baptized.

In preparation for the next session have each person write a short story explaining sin and forgiveness to an elementary school child. Read Chapter 5. Ask everyone to bring to class your church's most recent baptismal liturgy used in lesson one.

5. The Cleansing Bath

Share your short stories. Discuss them in the light of Chapter 5 and your church's baptismal liturgy.

In preparation for the next session have each person design a church putting the baptismal font where you believe it belongs. Also have each person draw a baptismal font as they would like to have it in his or her church. Use the pictures of fonts in this book for inspiration. Read Chapter 6.

6. All in the Family

Take a "field trip" to visit the baptismal font in your church. While you are there, share your church designs and font pictures. Compare and contrast your different visual conceptions in the light of Chapter 6. Discuss how you might redesign your church to make baptisms more meaningful.

In preparation for the next session, write your reflections about the story of Jesus' baptism in Luke 3:1-22 or Matthew 3:1-17. Read Chapter 7.

7. You've Got Spirit

Share your reflections about Jesus' baptism and discuss them in the light of Chapter 7. Together make one or more banners on the theme of the Holy Spirit and baptism.

In preparation for the next session have each person ask at least six persons "Are you born again?" Ask each person to explain what they mean? Read Chapter 8.

8. How to Be Born Again

Share the results of your interviews and discuss them in the light of Chapter 8. Then have each person share with the group his or her faith biography, that is, how he or she became the person of faith he or she now is.

In preparation for the next session, read Romans 6:1-14. What do you think Paul means when he says "In baptism we are buried with Christ"? Why is baptism related to death? Read Chapter 9.

9. Death by Drowning

Discuss how baptisms are celebrated in your church in the light of this chapter. Discuss ways that the meaning of baptism as death and rebirth might be made a more dramatic experience in your church. Prepare a presentation for your church council, vestry, session, or administrative board recommending changes in the way you perform baptisms.

In preparation for the last session, have each person write a paragraph explaining "who you are." Read Chapter 10.

10. Remember Who You Are

Share your paragraphs and discuss them in the light of Chapter 10. Then develop an educational program for parents which members from your class might offer to give parents who desire their children to be baptized. Share your program with your pastor. Ask your pastor to close your session with a service of renewal of your baptismal vows and communion.

Index of Scripture

Old Testament

New Testament